Unlocking Your BRILLIANCE

SMART STRATEGIES for **WOMEN** to THRIVE

in **SCIENCE, TECHNOLOGY, ENGINEERING,** and **MATH**

KAREN D. PURCELL, P.E.

GREENLEAF
BOOK GROUP PRESS

Published by Greenleaf Book Group Press
Austin, Texas
www.gbgpress.com

Distributed by Greenleaf Book Group LLC

For ordering information or special discounts for bulk purchases, please contact Greenleaf Book Group LLC at PO Box 91869, Austin, TX 78709, 512.891.6100.

Design and composition by Greenleaf Book Group LLC
Cover design by Greenleaf Book Group LLC

Cataloging-in-Publication data
(Prepared by The Donohue Group, Inc.)
Purcell, Karen D.
  Unlocking your brilliance : smart strategies for women to thrive in science, technology, engineering, and math / Karen D. Purcell. -- 1st ed.
    p. ; cm.
  Includes bibliographical references.
  ISBN: 978-1-60832-376-0
  1. Women in the professions. 2. Women--Employment. 3. Career development. 4. Success in business. I. Title.
HD6054 .P87 2012
331.48   2012935802

Part of the Tree Neutral® program, which offsets the number of trees consumed in the production and printing of this book by taking proactive steps, such as planting trees in direct proportion to the number of trees used: www.treeneutral.com

Printed in the United States of America on acid-free paper

12 13 14 15 16 17   10 9 8 7 6 5 4 3 2 1

First Edition

TreeNeutral

To my husband, Jeff,
and daughters, Alyssa and Sydney –
Thank you for your endless support and love.

CONTENTS

PREFACE   VII

INTRODUCTION   1

CHAPTER 1
Start Early, Keep with It   9

CHAPTER 2
Thrive in the Company of Men   29

CHAPTER 3
Find the Right Career Path   45

CHAPTER 4
Do the Work Well and Respect Will Follow   63

CHAPTER 5
Move On Up—and Love It   79

CHAPTER 6
Hold Your Head High   97

CHAPTER 7
Believe in Having It All   111

CHAPTER 8
Looking Forward   133

CONCLUSION   141

BIBLIOGRAPHY   143

ABOUT THE AUTHOR   147

PREFACE

After deliberating for many years about what I have to offer by sharing my story as a female electrical engineer, I was finally convinced, *by men*, to put my story in writing. I made this decision while attending, of all things, one of the largest gatherings of sports fanatics from across the world: the Winter Olympics. I found myself attending the men's hockey tournament of the 2010 Vancouver Winter Games with the other eight members in my Entrepreneurs' Organization (EO) forum—all men. The experience was surreal. I shared second row seats with the most successful business owners I know, some of the people I respect most in my life.

The Olympic environment was explosive. The camaraderie among the different countries lifted us. Each country's fans wore their location-specific colors, sang hearty chants, and exuded national pride. They were there to offer boundless support to the people they believed in. Through the common goals they shared, the various countries found common bonds and worked together. The environment and culture mirrored the philosophy of our forum and, ultimately, of EO. We support one another, help one another fulfill our life dreams, share common goals, and, most important, strongly believe in each of our members. Although we have yet to paint our faces and strut through the streets wearing EO's flag as a cape, we hold every bit as much passion as the hockey fans we sat among.

That night, on our drive back to the American side of the border, we stopped at a restaurant just outside of Vancouver, British Columbia. Throughout that memorable dinner I kept marveling at how I had earned my spot at this table of successful entrepreneurs, and I felt extremely proud.

Let me roll the clock back a bit to show how I came to arrive at such a place and such a question. In 2006 I joined EO, a business network that spans the globe, with a membership of more than eight thousand business owners in forty countries. Committing to a solid network such as the one this organization supplies has been vital to my success as a business owner. And, although the network is not specific to women, it has helped me grow as a *female* electrical engineer and business owner, which is a major part of who I am.

When it came time for our forum to select a destination for our 2010 annual retreat, the group decided to give the responsibility to me and forum chair Dave Sinclair, who is the president and founder of a successful alarm company. Our forum was the sum of a recent merger between two smaller forums. When the two merged, we adopted a tradition that one of the smaller forums had of keeping the retreat destination a secret. So, when Dave and I first met in October, we kept our discussions confidential. The other members discussed possibilities with one another and pleaded with us for any details, but our lips were sealed.

When I brought to Dave's attention that the Winter Olympics would be in full force during the weekend designated for the retreat, he lit up. We agreed to look at the schedule of the games and pick something that would excite everyone. We went with the national sport of the host country and the largest event: the men's hockey tournament.

As soon as tickets were available to Americans, we bought nine for a Friday afternoon game between reigning world champion Sweden and Belarus. After buying the tickets, we decided to plan the rest of the trip around the game. We booked airfare, lodging, and transportation—all without revealing anything to the other members.

As the trip approached, we gave the members all the information they needed to know: be at the airport Thursday morning at 10:00 a.m. and bring your passport. Up until we handed out the boarding passes, no one knew our destination for the weekend. Plus, because the tickets showed that we were flying into Seattle, the group believed our telling them to bring their passports had simply been a ruse. No one knew we would jaunt up to Vancouver, let alone attend an Olympic event.

Dave and I had rented a beautiful home right on the ocean in Seattle because we wanted to have quick access to all that the Emerald City has to offer: restaurants, entertainment, shopping, street markets, and ocean views. I remember Mike Kitson taking pictures of a whale breaching right outside the house, for example. After a day of discussing EO business and a relaxed dinner, Dave and I pulled out a box for the members to tear into. Inside were nine red and blue USA sweatshirts along with nine commemorative tickets with the iconic Olympic Rings printed on them. The men, shouting and cheering like boys, were clearly excited.

On Friday morning the limo we had reserved picked us up and drove the two hours north to Vancouver. Initially, Dave and I thought a limo ride would simply be a novelty, but the time together to and from Vancouver proved to have a huge impact on our forum. With no member having the responsibility of driving,

we were able to conduct necessary forum business and also social-
ize in a way the forum had never before done as a whole.

It was during the limo ride back to Seattle that the discussion
focused on how I came to own the largest electrical engineering
firm in northern Nevada. For the first half of the ride, I shared
some of the milestones that elevated my career to where it is today.
During dinner our conversation continued, and I concluded my
story when I came to a point I was sure everyone in the forum was
already familiar with. Almost immediately, John Coman and Mike
Kitson said in unison, "You should write a book."

Throughout that entire notable trip in the Pacific Northwest,
I often reflected on how I would ever have survived in my career
without the support of the men in my forum. I may not have found
the confidence or gathered the knowledge to overcome the many
obstacles that have presented themselves throughout my career
as a female owner of an electrical engineering firm. Surrounding
myself with their positive influence has helped me make crucial
decisions when I've been faced with choices that had the potential
to break my career. But, no matter how much credit I give to my
EO forum, I know my venture as a businesswoman surrounded by
men started long before I was introduced to the group. And that's
the story I want to share with you now.

INTRODUCTION

When a male enrolls in college and selects a major such as engineering, the reactions from family and friends alike range from "Congratulations," and "What area is most interesting to you?" to "That's impressive, good luck." When a female chooses engineering, the reactions she hears range from "Do you think you can handle it?" and "Why *that*?" to "Are you good enough at math?" When I first announced that I was going to study engineering in college, the reactions were no different. Male friends as well as female friends asked, "Really, why?" or "Do you know what you're getting yourself into?" It is somewhat ironic that the guys were the very same friends I had helped with assignments from freshman through senior year so they passed our math classes and graduated!

Why are careers in math and science male-dominated even today, when women—at least on paper—share the same freedoms as men? What is it about, say, physics that attracts men and repels women? Is testosterone a required variable for understanding inertia or balancing the Schrödinger equation? And in mechanical engineering, do you need a prostate to design and operate a centrifugal pump?

There is no easy way to explain why more women are not encouraged to follow these career paths. Some arguments assign blame to the media for fostering an image that scientists and mathematicians in our society are male. Other views place the blame on educators for directing men into those "manly" fields and women into traditionally acceptable "womanly" fields such as teaching and nursing, which supposedly fit our nurturing nature. Whatever the reasons, and no matter how complex they prove to be, they cannot be justified. There is no legitimate excuse for *anyone* not being encouraged to follow his or her passions in life because of gender.

Studies that have examined test scores for both sexes at a variety of ages suggest that academic performance is not the greatest obstacle for girls who want to study math, science, or engineering. The gender stereotypes instilled in girls' minds at an early age are the real dream killers. By the time girls reach their teenage years, they have already formed opinions about which occupations are appropriate for their sex. Young women sometimes decide to avoid engineering without knowing everything that engineering entails. That's because they are not encouraged to follow such a path and therefore are not exposed to it. While a young male with average mechanical and mathematical abilities is still likely to be encouraged to explore engineering, only young females with remarkable abilities are thought to be prepared for the field.

As a society, we learn about the world and advance our well-being through science. The United States may be known around the world for its higher education, but there isn't as strong a focus on educating scientists and engineers as there is in other countries. Recently, American policy analysts have voiced their concern about the "declining US share in world patenting and scientific publishing" (Hunt, 2010). One significant reason for our falling behind is that female students are not being encouraged—as they are abroad—to pursue career paths in science, technology, engineering, or math. If we want to attract the best and brightest minds into the fields that will move us forward, we can no longer look to only half of the population.

For this reason, it is important to confront gender stereotypes head-on, and long before young people are faced with declaring their majors at the college level. Without making efforts to break gender stereotypes, we face the consequence of limiting the potential of our youth—both female and male. If careers in all fields were truly open to both sexes, future generations would be encouraged to choose the careers that best match their interests and skills.

By maintaining certain fields as male-dominated, we are also allowing the culture within those fields to be established and maintained by men. Therefore, the males in math- and science-related institutions and workplaces will continue to foster cultures that only meet the needs of men. These male-oriented cultures are not inviting to women, and as a result, they deter young women from choosing fields in math and science even if they have exceptional abilities.

Even though engineering can be an uninviting culture, I decided that it was what I wanted to do and that I was not going to let discomfort stand in my way. When I first went to college, boys were hesitant to have girls as part of their study groups. I did not let it bother me. I figured that they were the ones who were missing out on the experience.

In the university setting, engineering used to be a discipline with loosely defined curricula. This was because so many career options were available to engineers. For example, with an electrical engineering degree you can do software development, electronic chip design, and power systems just to name a few. In my Entrepreneurs' Organization (EO) forum, three of us have electrical engineering degrees and we all do something completely different: one is involved in the financial industry, one is involved in the computer industry, and my firm works on building electrical systems such as lighting and power.

Many different fields hired (and still hire) engineers, so universities tended to teach broad concepts and leave employers to handle the highly specialized training. While this has changed somewhat, there is still a substantial gap between what constitutes engineering in higher education and what constitutes engineering in the workplace. This disconnect can dissuade students who prefer more hands-on work and do not have the patience to struggle through four years of work that is more textbook- and lecture-oriented. On the other side of the spectrum, once students graduate from college and enter the workforce, they may lack confidence in their technical skills. Both situations can cause students or recent graduates to exit the engineering field at the university or professional level more quick than students or recent graduates in other areas.

It has been my experience that school gives students a broad overview of their desired discipline. Only a handful of classes are applicable in daily work life, but university courses give the theory and knowledge behind the many applications. It is on-the-job training that becomes relevant. For example, I was never taught in school how to determine what lighting fixtures would be appropriate in a specific room, how to circuit or switch the light fixtures to provide different lighting levels, or how to calculate lighting levels. What I did learn was that the current flows from a power source to a switch and the current encounters resistance along the way to make the lighting fixtures operate. Once in the real world, I was required to learn the lighting calculations, lighting fixture selection, and how to circuit a room full of lighting fixtures on a set of plans in order to be successful in the workplace.

O—O—O

Throughout history, women have achieved tremendous accomplishments in the traditionally male-dominated fields of science, technology, engineering, and math—commonly referred to as the STEM fields. From elementary school through high school, I remember reading and studying about such accomplished women as Amelia Earhart, Juliette Gordon Low, and Sally Ride. I also recall visiting the United Nations in the summer of 1980 when I was a girl of twelve. The 1980s had been declared the UN Decade for Women. Through all my reading, I was amazed to discover the triumphs as well as hardships that women had faced. Women worked on the Manhattan Project, contributed to our understanding of DNA, discovered radium, and helped design and build the Golden Gate Bridge, just to name a few accomplishments. In addition to mastering difficult subjects and techniques of experimentation, however, these women also had to overcome the obstacle of a bias against their participation in and restricted access to STEM disciplines. Although that obstacle is less overt today, biases and restrictions still keep women from choosing STEM career paths in large numbers.

This book is for women who are thinking of pursuing a male-dominated major, those who are struggling with intimidation in the workforce, or those who simply need further encouragement to remain in their field. My aim is to limit the level of intimidation females experience while selecting their career paths, completing their schooling, working in their chosen fields, or owning their own businesses. For a woman, choosing or advancing her career already comes with added daily pressure and stress. Choosing or advancing her career in a field primarily composed of the opposite sex can be enough to break her spirit and have her banging her head against the wall. I hope *Unlocking Your Brilliance* will serve as a resource for women to find motivation to push forward (despite the pressures being applied by coworkers, bosses, society and, *gasp*, even their own families).

My point is not to view men as monsters. Rather, it is to see them as mentors, colleagues, and confidants. Women are not trying to flip the situation and dominate the careers in which men currently rule; we are merely trying to work beside them in equal numbers to advance the fields. After all, science is about critical thinking and taking risks in order to unveil knowledge—it is about learning all we can. Leveling the playing field will help crush the social stigma that says careers in science, technology, engineering, and mathematics are for boys only. Present day and future generations should be able to pursue their talents in any field, regardless of how many males or females are currently working in it.

Finding validation for our involvement in male-dominated careers can be extremely difficult; I know it was for me. Throughout this book I will share my story, highlight common hurdles that women in similar situations typically face, and offer insight into strategies that women can apply to overcome them. My hope is that this book can be a useful source of validation for any woman experiencing stress from her professional position in an environment that is primarily male. It is often useful to relate to someone else's story so we know our own struggles are not unprecedented. Although our numbers are minimal in the STEM fields, we are certainly not alone.

Chapter 1

START EARLY, KEEP WITH IT

I lived a typical childhood in a typical town—Harrisburg, Pennsylvania. I liked spectator sports, competing in field hockey, spending time with my friends, playing the clarinet in the marching band as well as concert band, and being with my family. I spent four to eight weeks of my summer every year from the ages of nine to sixteen away at summer camp where we would swim, play various sports, hike, and do a variety of art projects. As a family, we would spend a week of summer vacation in Wildwood, New Jersey, at the beach.

My parents stressed the importance of education, which suited me just fine because I enjoyed school. As far back as I can remember, I was interested in a variety of subjects, but math held my attention more than any of the others. In high school, I think that I helped the majority of the boys in my geometry, trigonometry, and calculus classes get through and pass. They would come over to my house so I could explain the math problems and help them with (or actually do) their homework. Through elementary school and middle school, this didn't separate me from other girls much, but as I began my high school career, excelling in math and science began to seem less girlie.

High school is such a challenging time. You are almost an adult, but not quite. You are trying to figure out what you want to be when you grow up and what classes are appropriate to take. And then you have the peer and societal pressures. Are you part of the right clique? You don't really want to be different than anyone else, yet you want to stand out to some extent. I remember high school as a fun time. I was fortunate to have a good group of girlfriends as well as boyfriends (friends that just happened to be boys). I learned time management at an early age. I split my time between my activities, my friends, and my studies. Math was very important to me, so I did not let anyone else's negative or positive comments change any of my actions or decisions. Looking back, I think a lot of girls were actually jealous of my math abilities and, because of that aptitude, my interaction with lots of boys.

Another important aspect of my life then was that I ended up meeting my first husband when I was a junior in high school. We actually met in a grocery store where some of my high school friends worked. He went to a different high school. Our relationship continued on through high school and added to the complexities of life at that time.

As high school progressed, the need to choose a career path loomed. Since I didn't want to scribble out equations in front of bored students for the rest of my life, the math route appeared to be a dead end. And while I loved playing field hockey, I was pretty certain that I couldn't make a living at it. So, like most high school students exploring what to do with their lives after graduation, I turned to teachers, peers, counselors, and my parents to discuss options. Various options were raised, including becoming a teacher or an accountant, but nothing really clicked with me or caused me to say, "Yes! That's what I want to do with my life."

My mother was a nurse at the local hospital. She is twenty-six years older than I am, and in her day, women predominantly pursued one of two career paths: nursing or teaching. Even though my mother's choices were narrow, she found fulfillment in becoming a nurse and was exceptional at it. In a different time, I have no doubt she could have completed med school and become a doctor. To this day people in her community call her for medical advice before they pay a visit to a physician. With that kind of medical talent in my immediate family, I'm not sure how I got stuck with the deathly-afraid-of-needles gene. Even as an adult, and mother of two, I still get queasy when I think about a meeting between any needle and my arm. For this reason alone, I knew the medical professions were not for me. Plus, it was the kind of traditional path I didn't find appealing.

My father was an entrepreneur who started a variety of small businesses and worked at making them successes. His influence would shine through later in my professional life, but majoring in "entrepreneur" wasn't a path of study at the time, so I didn't even consider it.

My parents encouraged my younger brother and me to be whatever we wanted to be in life. Still, no matter how free we were to dream and pick our own way, I still believed that college was my only option after high school. It did not seem so much an option as a requirement.

As I began the countdown to graduation day, counselors and teachers began asking me what my plans were for the future. *Where did I want to continue my schooling? What did I want to be? Was I sticking around Harrisburg?* I was disappointed that my guidance counselors and school administrators were not suggesting anything related to math or science. I thought at the time that my only option was to study math to become a math teacher. Not that there is anything wrong with becoming a teacher, but there I was, stuck with a decision similar to my mother's: Do I want to be a teacher or a nurse? Back in my high school years the Internet did not exist, so researching career options was very time-consuming and confusing. There didn't seem to be a lot of obvious choices. My high school physics teacher, a man, finally made a suggestion instead of posing another string of endless questions. He told me that, based on my aptitude in math and science, I should consider engineering, a career dominated—then and now—by males. I asked him what engineers do and his answer boiled down to "lots of things." I was so relieved that someone in an authoritative position, who was teaching a subject I liked and was good at, gave me that recommendation. I will never forget that teacher and will be eternally grateful to him. I guess, in hindsight, that was the point at which my life got complicated.

THE HURDLE: OVERCOMING THE LACK OF EXPOSURE

Gender stereotypes have always helped steer men and women toward separate paths. These stereotypes are ingrained into the minds of our youth by way of media, family life, education, and society. And these societal pressures have been a consistent focus of seemingly endless research. For instance, sociologist Alice Baumgartner-Papageorgiou surveyed two thousand eight- to seventeen-year-olds in 1982 to find out what career paths they would follow if they awoke the next morning as the opposite sex. Her study uncovered some amazing but not extremely surprising results.

The young girls frequently replied that they would be construction workers, athletes, pilots, and engineers. Had I been questioned as part of the survey, I would already have been inclined to want to be an engineer too. The girls said that, if male, they would likely be rich and enjoy more freedom while having less responsibility. They also remarked that they would show off more frequently, be more macho, not express their inner feelings, act calm and collected, and be more valued by their parents. Obviously the young females felt that they did not have the same opportunities that their male counterparts did.

The boys followed suit by submitting comments that further trapped females inside stereotypical roles. The young males surveyed frequently replied that they would be secretaries, airline stewardesses, teachers, or prostitutes. Boys also thought that they would get paid less and be expected to become homemakers. Baumgartner-Papageorgiou conducted the same study ten years later and collected similar results (Baumgartner-Papageorgiou, 1982, 1992).

Studies such as this highlight an interesting question: Would young women choose to follow a different career path for the rest of their lives if they were encouraged by society to make the decision based on their interests and skills?

As I just shared, over the course of my entire high school career, only one teacher recognized the aptitude I showed in math and science and looked beyond the fact that I was female to suggest that I follow a career path in one of the STEM fields. Although that was years and years ago, things have improved only so much today. And it gets to the underlying reason why there aren't more women in the STEM fields. Young girls cannot possibly consider opportunities they do not know exist. If girls are not exposed to certain career paths, particularly STEM careers, prior to or during high school, they are highly unlikely to elect to follow them in college.

Stephen Hegedus, PhD, is the founding director of the Kaput Center for Research and Innovation in STEM Education at the University of Massachusetts Dartmouth. He argues that girls are not as comfortable as boys are when deciding to pursue their strengths in science and math because girls "have not been educated or mentored to follow STEM career pathways as much as boys" (Lade, 2011). The American Association of University Women and the National Science Foundation have published a host of statistics that back up this claim: Approximately 66 percent of young children indicate they like science, but once they enter middle school, girls and boys differ in their attitudes about and interests in science. And even though girls take as many science classes in high school as boys do, many of them don't continue their studies as undergraduates (Dyer, 2004; National Science Foundation, 2007).

Lack of early exposure can be detrimental to achieving gender balance in STEM fields because such degrees typically require students to get on the right path prior to freshman year. The studies are intensive and usually begin in the very first semester of college. Young adults are inquisitive and may end up in STEM fields for a variety of reasons, but early exposure to these fields would result in more informed and more precise decisions when selecting a college or university and a particular course of study. More than that, it would help young women understand that their gender shouldn't determine the career path they choose and that pursuing a STEM career doesn't make them any less feminine.

For example, it is possible to be a successful career woman and still have a family. In 2010, China actually required that its female astronauts also be mothers. In the United States, one female high achiever in a STEM field is Lisa P. Jackson. She was appointed by President Barack Obama as the current head of the Environmental Protection Agency. This amazing woman earned a masters degree in chemical engineering and is the proud mother of two (Wikipedia, 2012).

When I talked to other female engineers in my area as I was writing this book, I found out that they felt the same about poor STEM exposure prior to or during high school. One young woman told me she always dreamed of being an astronaut and believed an engineering degree was a reasonable place to start, which it can be. However, once she settled into mechanical engineering she found an area she was very interested in and now happily works for a private firm in Reno that provides plumbing and mechanical (heating, ventilating, and air-conditioning, or HVAC) system design for commercial projects such as hospitals, schools, and airports.

A coworker of mine is now one of the top designers of electrical systems in Nevada after selecting (and quickly deselecting) biology in college. Another friend of mine believed throughout childhood and high school that she wanted to be an architect. She planned on pursuing a career in architecture until a friend of hers with some engineering knowledge mentioned that her interests aligned more with engineering. After taking a break from schooling to decide what she really wanted to do, my friend decided her true passion was civil engineering. Today she not only works for a well-respected civil engineering firm, she also visits high schools through a program with the American Society of Civil Engineers to speak about the field and the opportunities that can be found within it.

Had these women been exposed to their chosen fields earlier on in their lives, they would have been better armed to select a path that matched their true interests. They all ended up finding their calling eventually and are now very happy. But how many other women failed to stumble upon the career path that could have been their true calling because they were not exposed to STEM fields? This is a loss both to those individuals and to the professions.

Having grown up in the 1960s, Pamela Brown, dean of the School of Arts and Sciences at the New York City College of Technology and a chemical engineer, was inspired by the international space race, which led to her enrollment in a two-week summer course on astronomy at the University of California, Los Angeles. Only seven years old at the time, Pamela became "completely hooked" on pursuing a STEM career. "By the time I got to high school, I was one of the few females in honors math. I had a particularly chauvinistic math teacher in ninth grade, and, rather than tolerate his attitude, I asked to be transferred to a different, more supportive instructor."

Even at the young age of fourteen, Pamela says, "I felt I was entitled to a supportive learning environment." But the request for a class transfer was met with some resistance. "Initially," she recalls, "the guidance counselor said no to the change in teacher, so my mother went over his head to the principal and arranged for the change. She argued that I was a good student, and if I thought I needed the change, then she supported me. He agreed. I continued to love math and excel in the subject."

"Trust your instincts when you feel that you are not in a good learning environment," Pamela advises, "and try to do something about it. I could have given up, decided to become a troublemaker, or tolerated the negativity. Instead, I arranged for another teacher."

Science and technology are and will continue to be important factors in what we are able to accomplish in our lifetimes. As long as young boys and girls are exposed to science and technology and equally encouraged to study those disciplines, those with talent and a genuine interest in those fields will be able to develop that interest. Concerning technology, for instance, there are documented differences in girls' and boys' preferences. Boys, in general, tend to enjoy exploring technology simply for technology's sake. They like playing games on or tinkering with computers just for the fun involved. Girls, on the other hand, want to know what the technology can do and use it as a means to accomplish certain purposes. For example, girls use technology to find information or to maintain social relationships (Farmer, 2009). These inherent differences are a positive thing. By having both mind-sets working to advance technology and the fields that use it, we better our overall chances of accomplishing amazing feats.

As a country, we stand to gain a lot by exposing young girls to STEM fields and encouraging those who are interested to follow their hearts and minds.

Simply focusing attention on one age group cannot cure all societal issues that influence career choices among females. Correcting the negative perceptions that girls develop at a young age can, however, lead them to not avoid math and science when they reach high school. Administrators and educators must strive to create environments in high school and college math and science programs that are inviting to females to help prevent the likelihood of their choosing a different direction.

Luckily for me, my perceptive high school physics teacher suggested that engineering could be the right fit for me. Nevertheless, my lack of exposure to engineering in high school continued to have an adverse impact as I selected my major, earned my engineering degree, and pursued my career after graduation. It seemed that my professors and advisors at every turn assumed I was already knowledgeable about the different areas of the discipline—boy, were they wrong! I didn't even know how much I didn't know, and I also didn't know what questions to ask to elicit the information I needed. Needless to say, I was uncertain, confused, and frustrated.

Even though I found my way to an engineering degree and career, I would have dealt with less uncertainty had I experienced greater exposure to the subject before or during high school. My lack of knowledge blurred my decision-making abilities until my career was well under way.

If I had struggled with my studies or had any other hesitations, this added uncertainty could have tipped the scales. I might never have completed my degree or have moved into the career I now love so much. Consequently, in conjunction with writing this book, I am also launching STEMspire, a nonprofit focused on encouraging girls and young women to explore and remain in STEM fields. A portion of the proceeds of book sales will go toward offering scholarships for their studies within any of the four STEM disciplines.

STRATEGIES FOR MAKING IT THROUGH

So what's a girl to do? The following are some tips for empowering yourself regardless of the level of information or exposure that's readily available.

⊘ Seek out special programs inside or outside of school

More and more workshops are sprouting up nowadays that encourage young girls to maintain their interest in STEM fields.

A friend of mine, Lynda Wiest, who teaches math education at the University of Nevada, recently published a paper in which she noted that out-of-school-time programs focusing on females in mathematics "are increasing in number as well as in the professional and public attention they receive." She went on to write, "The number of such programs for girls increased 140 percent in less than a decade" (Wiest, 2010). The idea of offering STEM-focused programs to young females outside of school is becoming a popular strategy—one I wish had been explored much more when I was a youngster.

One organization with a strong focus on increasing STEM-field interest among young people is the Institute for Mathematics and Computer Science (IMACS), an independent institute located in Plantation, Florida. In a recent article published on the organization's website, a staff writer encouraged parents of girls with interests in math and science to expose their daughters to an out-of-school program with a STEM focus. "When a girl is surrounded by other girls who are also interested in these subjects, then being a 'math and science girl' doesn't seem so 'out there,' and the stereotype that STEM is for boys is less likely to be reinforced" (IMACS, 2011).

The decision to follow a STEM education path (and eventually a STEM career path) is a major decision. The Internet—which, unfortunately, was nonexistent when I was in grade school—is a tremendous resource for helping young girls explore STEM. If you or someone you know is a young female interested in finding out more about STEM opportunities, I urge you to take a look at the following list of organizations that offer guidance and information. These organizations offer a wide range of programs from very challenging and sophisticated to sheer fun and creative. Even the old standby the YWCA is keeping pace with the modern world in their program offerings, so don't rule such agencies out as stodgy. Don't be dissuaded from pursuing your passions for any reason, especially not because of a lack of exposure or outdated perceptions.

⊘ Find opportunities in the community to learn more about STEM careers

As shown in the list on the next page, even such popular national clubs as Girl Scouts of the USA have started to give added attention to introducing girls to STEM. Having been a troop leader for the past several years, I have noticed an improved focus on motivating young girls to explore typically male-dominated fields. This shows an important shift in thinking since the days when I was a Girl Scout. Back then, we worked on such traditional badges as cooking and health. These are still important, but today the organization has really stepped up its programs to help ensure that girls succeed in all areas. It even has a program that is dedicated to STEM. Within that program, the Girl Scouts have "Imagine Engineering," which gives an overview of the types of job duties engineers commonly perform, and "FIRST Robotics." "FIRST" stands for "For Inspiration and Recognition of Science and Technology." This platform inspires girls to become science and technology leaders (Girl Scouts of the USA, 2012). I wish these programs had been available to me in my girlhood.

Once we enter college, we can investigate opportunities for summer internships to learn more about different possibilities in the field we're studying. As a matter of fact, even during high school we can seek out those same opportunities. By working with our guidance counselors, we can identify a list of companies (even if it's a very short one) that operate in the fields in which we're

NATIONAL PROGRAMS FOR YOUNG WOMEN INTERESTED IN STEM FIELDS

→ Aspire—sponsored by the Society of Women Engineers (SWE)

→ Digigirlz—offered by Microsoft

→ Girls' Electronic Mentoring in Science, Engineering and Technology (GEM-SET)

→ Girls Incorporated Thinking SMART Program

→ Girls, Math & Science Partnership (GMSP)

→ Girl Scouts of the USA

→ Inspiring Girls Now in Technology Evolution (IGNITE)

→ My Gifted Girl

→ National Girls Collaborative Project (NGCP)

→ Sally Ride Science

→ YWCA

interested, like engineering companies, construction companies that employ engineers, technology companies, research organizations, and the like. We just have to take action and contact them to find out if they're in need of free labor from somebody who thinks she would like to work in that field someday. Many firms also now offer job shadowing programs or career days. Job shadowing allows those interested in a specific field to follow for a day or a given amount of time an individual who is already working in that field. This lets the individual see typical job duties and activities required for that field. It is a great way to get a feel for what a job may entail.

⊘ Find a mentor

At an early age, if we feel like we aren't getting the advice or information we need to make the right decision, it may be time to seek out a mentor. This may be a person from school, in the community, or from a national organization. Below is a list of organizations that can help connect interested young women with mentors.

Association for Women in Mathematics (AWM)

Association of Women in Science (AWIS)

Institute of Electrical and Electronic Engineers (IEEE)

National Academy of Engineering (NAE)

National Academy of Sciences (NAS)

National Center for Women and Information Technology (NCWIT)

National Society of Professional Engineers (NSPE)

Society of Women Engineers (SWE)

Women in Technology International (WITI)

In the college environment, many of these organizations have university chapters or local mentoring programs. While finding a female mentor may help us understand what it will be like to enter a certain field, any professional, male or female, will be able to share information that will help us make better decisions.

Mary Fernandez, board chairman of MentorNet and assistant vice president of research at AT&T Labs, got into mentoring students because she had such a great mentor at AT&T Bell Labs. "What I've observed," Mary said, "is that others can see potential in you that you cannot see in yourself. If they articulate it to you, you simply might not believe it. I think women suffer from this more than men. There's a lot of literature that says men tend to be overconfident in what they know, while women tend to be underconfident."

Mentors also offer challenges or opportunities. "On the inside, you might be saying: 'Oh my God, I'm completely unqualified for this,'" said Mary. "But even if your internal voice is saying no, it's important that you go ahead and do it anyway. Humble yourself to people who can be your champions and advisors. They can help you fill in the blanks of any knowledge that you might not have. In the end, the potential that your mentor saw in you will be realized simply by you doing the job. You have to be willing to move out of your comfort zone."

Mary wishes that the gender disparity in STEM fields didn't exist for so many reasons, "including the importance of technology to society, and the future of the planet," she said. "But as long as that disparity exists, women have a disproportionate opportunity to influence their STEM field. Because we're different. And that's a good thing; it's not a disadvantage, even though it might be a challenge at times.

"When your internal voice is giving you a lot of second-guessing," Mary concluded, "make sure you also spend time listening to the external voices. Don't shy away from opportunities—embrace them, even if they sound scary."

⊘ Take charge and get informed

Today, vast resources are available online for women interested in STEM fields. You can visit the websites of any of the organizations I just mentioned or the programs listed earlier and learn a great deal about the particular field that interests you, about what it's like to be a woman in a STEM profession, about career opportunities, and so on. While it might not be as enlightening as face-to-face communication with a professional, it will certainly give you a good starting point.

More important, though, you have to decide to take charge of your career destiny early, particularly in the STEM fields. Tracy Drain, a systems engineer with NASA's Jet Propulsion Laboratory, learned this crucial lesson from her mother, to whom she is eternally grateful. When Tracy received an F on her sixth-grade science class progress report, it might have seemed that she wasn't exactly cut out for a future career in a STEM field. But looking back, Tracy now realizes that her adolescent self simply lacked focus, which included forgetting homework assignments and not always bothering to study for tests.

Tracy dreaded her parents' reaction to the failing grade. But instead of getting mad or punishing her, Tracy's mother simply pointed out that the ways in which Tracy performed in her early school years could impact the rest of her life—stressing that it was solely up to her to turn things around. "I remember being completely dumbfounded," said Tracy. "I don't even know if I said anything back to her at all, or just stumbled off to my room. My mom had told me before why school was important, but I think I had never, *ever* thought about it like that before."

Immediately, Tracy set herself on a new, more focused academic path—leading to honors-level grades from middle school on through to the end of high school. She said her one regret is that she didn't more thoroughly research the exact GPA requirements for earning the most lucrative college scholarships. "Everyone should shoot for the best grades they can get," she pointed out, "while realizing that grades aren't the be-all and end-all, of course. But if you know early on where the key break-points are, it's easier to know when you are starting to go off track, so you can seek additional help to get back on target."

CONCLUSION

Fueled by the social movements of the 1960s, agencies in our federal government tried to neutralize gender bias within the STEM disciplines. In 1972, for example, an educational amendment prohibited sexual discrimination in all educational programs that accepted federal assistance. But the ban did not immediately implant a gender-neutral system across all fields. It took the Women's Educational Equity Act in 1974 to build upon the education amendments of 1972 and call for the development of educational programs, materials, and practices that were designed to help women achieve educational equality (US Department of Labor, 2010).

And, although I was just an elementary school girl in the mid-1970s, amendments and acts like these paved the way for me to choose an area of STEM to study. These measures were relatively recent. Plus, they only called for institutions to implement practices that aimed at increasing gender equality in education; they did not address issues outside of education, such as gender equality in the workplace.

Without understanding the opportunities that are available to students of math and science, young women may think they have made a mistake when facing the challenges of completing a STEM major. The good news is that current programs that focus on increasing young girls' interest in those fields are tremendous. But without them, there are potential long-term consequences, even for girls who select a STEM path in college.

While young people today have opportunities to become exposed to more STEM subjects than were available when I was in high school, still more needs to be done. Out-of-school programs are gaining popularity, and in order for that to continue, those of us in STEM fields have to support both local and national efforts to foster girls. The United States is trailing behind other countries in the STEM fields because fewer young people are pursuing STEM degrees in college. This will continue to plague our country until students have adequate opportunities to explore math and science throughout elementary, middle, and high school.

For inspiration, tools, and resources, visit www.UnlockingYourBrilliance.com and www.STEMspire.org.

Chapter 2

THRIVE IN THE COMPANY OF MEN

My young eyes bright with naïveté, off I went in search of a university that offered an engineering major. I could always change majors later if I didn't like it, right? The university also had to meet my crucial criteria: be close enough to home that I could visit when I wanted yet be far enough away that I couldn't do so every day. With its two-hour-away driving distance, Widener University in Chester, Pennsylvania, was the school where I chose to begin my freshman year.

Although I had applied and was accepted to about half a dozen schools, Widener attracted me because of its size and culture. Located on the Delaware River just outside of Philadelphia, Chester rang through with the sports-town feel and historical qualities I loved about the City of Brotherly Love. The people were loyal to the area and cheered adamantly for the Phillies on a fall afternoon, the Flyers at night, the 76ers through the winter and spring, the Nittany Lions on Saturdays, and the Eagles on Sundays. Keeping pace with my sports-crazed surroundings, I competed in field hockey—a sport I had started playing competitively in high school. My relationship with my high school boyfriend had ended (temporarily). He entered the US Air Force and I was at Widener, about to embark on engineering.

I was familiar with the area, but I still was not sure what I was there to do. I went to my advisor in search of some advising. "What can I do with an engineering degree?" I asked.

"Just try your first semester and see if you like it," he replied. As elementary as his advice seemed at the time, looking back it was probably the best advice I ever received as a coed. So, I chose engineering as my broad major and began my first round of college courses.

As you'll recall my admitting in chapter one, I always liked school, and university studies were no exception. I finished my first semester with a 4.0. Up to that point, I was happy with the courses even though they were fairly general. Because I already knew by that point that my advisors lacked any truly helpful or specific advice, I made the decision alone to continue my second semester on the path toward a bachelor's degree in engineering.

As early on as my freshman year, I noticed the gender imbalance in the entry-level engineering courses I was taking. Widener's class sizes were about one hundred strong in the lecture-based courses and a bit smaller in the hands-on courses. Most of my lectures carried a 9:1 male-to-female ratio. But, because everyone merely sat and took notes for the most part, the imbalance was not an issue; we were all equal as student note-takers, after all.

In many of the hands-on courses, we were required to break into teams in order to complete a number of projects. It was then that I started recognizing some of the biases the male students had toward the females. For some reason, the men (*boys* might be the more appropriate word in this context) had it in their minds that the females were beneath them in terms of skills. Typically we would form our own study groups or create our own lab teams. The boys would just shy away from us and stick to a "boys only" group. From the boys' behavior, I surmised it was ingrained in their heads that we young women could not possibly be strong in math or science. I knew females made up a small portion of the engineering students at Widener (and beyond), but up to this point, I had yet to experience any true gender bias from male students. This was the first time I was exposed to this hurdle.

And I didn't like it one bit. I was annoyed by their closed-mindedness and really felt like running my straight–A report card under their noses.

THE HURDLE: FACING THE REALITY OF GENDER IMBALANCE

In the small study groups that quickly developed, I noticed the boys were hesitant to invite female classmates to join. Or, when they did invite us, they did not take our input seriously. In study groups, we females were required to prove our capabilities, whereas the males were given a free pass because of their gender. The boys believed the other boys held the same skills, but the girls were thought to be lost or behind in the material. This was frustrating because I had to keep wasting time proving myself every time I joined a new group. It was an unwelcome stress I started to anticipate each time I thought of joining others to study. I think the boys realized that I was a valuable asset to their group shortly after our first exam in each class. They would see that I would get a good grade when maybe they did not. Over time, they slowly but surely realized that I should have been a part of their group from day one!

Unfortunately, the bias of our male colleagues is simply a reflection of the bias of our society as a whole. While it has changed substantially in the past twenty or thirty years, there is still a sense that women aren't as good at math, for instance, even though there is almost no evidence to support such a belief.

In high schools today, boys and girls earn almost the same number of credits in math and science. In fact, girls earn a bit more than boys, according to the report "Why So Few? Women in Science, Technology, Engineering, and Mathematics" from the American Association of University Women and supported by the National Science Foundation (NSF). And girls, on average, are earning higher GPAs in math and science than are boys (Corbett et al., 2010).

Sadly, even though the actual differences in performance are minimal or nonexistent, when they are presented with biased information, women actually perform at a lower level. In a compelling study described within "Why So Few?" researchers found that suggesting that men or women perform better in a certain area actually makes men or women perform better. They divided study participants who all held similar skills in math into two groups, telling one group that, statistically, men performed better on the test they were about to take and the other group that men and women typically performed equally well. "Their results were starkly different: In the group told that men do better, men indeed did much better, with an average score of 25 compared with the women's 5. In the group told there was no difference, women scored 17 and men 19" (Lewin, 2010).

An abundance of articles has disproved the notion that males are naturally better at math, but some researchers continue to see validity in the argument. This is because even though the majority of available research shows that boys and girls have basically equal mathematical ability, boys still do outscore girls at the very high end of math score distribution. Therefore, some researchers believe that once men and women enroll in very specific classes or enter certain careers that are extremely demanding mathematically, men are better suited to meet the demands. This could account for a limited number of special situations, but it does not help to explain the overall imbalance within STEM areas in college *and* beyond.

STRATEGIES FOR MAKING IT THROUGH

Leaving high school and entering college is one of the most life-changing transitions a young person experiences. Currently, more young women than young men choose to pursue a college degree. However, these numbers do not translate into the STEM fields, where men still dominate. According to the NSF, about one in every three males chooses to major in a STEM field, whereas only about one in twelve females chooses to do so.

Females usually underestimate their abilities in math and science, whereas males tend to overestimate theirs. Therefore, a young woman who approaches a field that has long been male-dominated must be enormously confident, unlike her male peers, who have a somewhat natural confidence when it comes to enrolling in challenging STEM classes. Young women can gain some of that confidence, and become well qualified, by taking advanced-placement courses in high school.

The college environment is rife with new challenges and experiences—some pleasant, some not. Encountering a strong bias simply because of our gender can be damaging to our psyches. Early in college, no one is positive about following the "right" path. Detractors can add to the self-doubt we experience as we try to accomplish our goals in an environment in which we are significantly outnumbered.

So what's a girl to do? The following are some strategies I uncovered for keeping your momentum in college even as gender imbalance and bias become real issues.

☑ Don't avoid 'em; join 'em

It's important to not further isolate ourselves by avoiding working with male classmates. When we enter into courses for any STEM discipline, the most notable challenges we'll face are typically of the social variety. Whether our male classmates are subtle or overt with their disapproval of us being in "their" program, we will have to get past it in order to succeed in our chosen fields. Instead of isolating ourselves from them, we should join them. While our relatively few female classmates can offer support and friendship because they understand what we are going through better than anyone, bonding with our male counterparts also has its distinct advantages.

Making efforts to bridge the gender gap can help establish our sense of belonging among the majority. As humans—and possibly even more so as women—we cannot ignore that we have the inherent need to belong. One basic place to start fostering relationships with our male classmates is with those who appear, right from the start, to be perfectly comfortable working with females. There will be at least a small handful of these males, and they are easy to find because they will often invite us to join their groups and conversations. We should not fear being rejected by a few disapproving men while attempting to identify and build relationships with the ones who are easygoing about working with both genders. It is to our benefit to invite men to join our groups and conversations. This can be challenging, especially if you are shy. Keeping in mind that men are people too will help you in this situation. In my experience, since there were so few of us women studying engineering, we all stuck together. The school that I went to was small, so everyone knew everyone. Relationships were built over time and it became easier to have a coed group. Once we have a group composed of students of both genders, our networking opportunities will widen.

As we network in our classes, we can draw on our inherently female characteristics—the ability to empathize and engage others, to acquire knowledge and ask for help, among others—as strengths. We can be social by asking male students about their studies, their interests, and their opinions. Since they, too, are surrounded by males, they will likely welcome the opportunity to have meaningful social interactions. It will be damaging if we only "talk shop" as a way to prove we belong. Through school and beyond, it can be frustrating to have to prove our abilities to others who doubt we possess them simply because we wear makeup and skirts, but we cannot let the frustrations keep us from being human. After all, the majority of our classmates may be male, but that does not disqualify them from being human.

Networking with males outside of class is also highly beneficial. It is natural for students to have a physical and sexual attraction to one another. This can be both positive and negative. On the positive side, relationships help with getting to know members of the opposite sex and allow both parties to express their opinions and knowledge with each other. It may make it easier to form study groups (some of his friends, some of her friends). On the flip side, it can complicate matters if the relationship turns ugly. It can lead to disrespect for each other and for members of the opposite sex. Sexual harassment can also be a concern. I was fortunate to never experience this while in school. Know the warning signs and report sexual harassment to an authoritative figure if you suspect it.

Sometimes, more insidious than overt sexual harrassment is subtle sexual discrimination. Nancy Knowlton, Sant Chair for Marine Science at the Smithsonian Institute and former board member of the American Association for the Advancement of Science, observed the effect such when she found herself at a conference in the U.K. where essentially all of the speakers were men. "The exceptions were all American citizens, or were brought up in the United States," she said. "The plenary speaker talked about having gotten the idea for his talk while washing the Christmas dinner dishes, having given his wife 'a much-deserved break.' Someone else showed a picture of his research assistant holding an animal, all that was visible was a set of hands with fingernail polish."

Nancy hadn't experienced sexism in the United States. She was so shocked by these incidents that she wrote a letter of protest to the related society journal. "My letter generated a lot of response. Interestingly enough, the next year the president was a woman!"

Early on in my program, I was constantly finding myself in male-dominated activities outside of class. For instance, instead of joining a sorority, I was a little sister in a fraternity. This was a social fraternity on campus; it was like having a family away from home. During my time in college, I was the only little sister that was an engineering major. Plenty of the guys were engineering or science majors, but no other women were. Whether I knew it or not, an activity such as this gave me courage to hold my own when I was outnumbered, underappreciated, or doubted in the classroom. Instead of avoiding situations where I was on the wrong end of the gender imbalance, I exposed myself to them in order to somewhat desensitize and adapt. To be candid about it, however, in reality I was expending a tremendous amount of energy constantly proving myself as capable among groups of bullheaded boys. (In the next strategies section, I'll share with you how that took its toll on me emotionally and physically.)

⊘ Be encouraged by your accomplishments

Reflecting on my own undergraduate experiences, I recall how the general mood of my male classmates shifted as they progressed through their degrees. Many of them became more boastful as they gained more education. Each semester's achievements reinforced in their minds that they had what it took to become engineers. The female students, on the other hand, did not seem to accept their progression as validation of their worthiness, even as they accomplished the same milestones. As students—regardless of our gender—each of us must accept and be encouraged by our achievements; every course we pass is another reason to celebrate that we are moving through a difficult program.

I learned that lesson the hard way. Early on in my program, students were unfamiliar with one another and with the course load; we all seemed to be a little lost, so any sort of real bias had yet to become an issue. But by the second semester of my sophomore year, I had made it through the weeding-out process that naturally develops because of the intense amount of math involved in all flavors of engineering. Instead of recognizing my accomplishment, I only feared what was to come.

Only students who proved they could handle the math load took courses during my sophomore year. Those who couldn't either dropped out or changed majors. I found myself surrounded almost entirely by males in courses that were quickly becoming more hands-on, team-oriented, and specific to engineering. It took nearly two years to prove to a handful of my male classmates that I was capable. Some of them were now asking me for help with their homework and taking what I had to say somewhat seriously. Even though it was a relatively small number of males who were finally opening up and accepting me, I should have recognized that as reinforcement that I was doing something right. Instead of being proud of the progress I was making, however, I focused on the larger number of males who found more arbitrary reasons to hold their heads higher than us females. Looking back, I realize this was a bitter perspective to have.

I remember the boys in my program becoming somewhat cocky as we approached our third year of the program. As students, we believed that by making it to our junior year in an engineering program, we (boys *and* girls) had demonstrated enough mathematical skill to earn an engineering degree. Yet, the male engineering students still refused to treat females as equal, even though we had completed the same courses. I still do not know what surprised me more: the idea that freshman men held freshman women to lower expectations even before any of us had received formal training, or the idea that three-quarters of the way through the degree program many of the males still felt that they had somehow done more to earn their positions. In both time frames, I wish I had focused more on the progress I was making rather than being frustrated with something that was well outside my control. I remember starting to feel really out of place and discouraged in my classes once I further narrowed my focus by selecting my emphasis: electrical engineering.

It was at the beginning of my junior year that I began to feel completely out of control. I was still unsure whether I had made the right decision by choosing to pursue engineering. I was in the middle of an extremely demanding degree program, surrounded by biased and boisterous male classmates, and constantly searching for reinforcement that everything was going to work out. I felt powerless to make a change even if I had wanted to; I was stuck. The feeling of disempowerment was overwhelming. The pressure became too much, and I developed an unhealthy eating disorder.

Over time, my friends started to notice my strange behavior and my unhealthy body. They went to the student health center and got information on what they could do to help. They also did a form of intervention to try to help me with this issue. In my opinion, a person needs to want to be helped and it can't be forced. At first, I didn't want to be helped. I thought I was in complete control. Eventually I realized that I wasn't in control, I needed and wanted help, and that my erratic behavior had to stop. My friends were there to support me and I am forever grateful.

Having very strict regulations about what I could eat was my way of finding a sense of control over something, *anything*. In our college cafeteria, I first limited myself to just the salad bar. Soon, I eliminated 99 percent of those offerings and refused to eat anything but shredded carrots. It got so bad that my skin was actually turning orange and I was exhausted all the time. I knew

I couldn't survive on the sustenance provided by a strictly carrot diet, but the sense of control that my eating disorder gave me was too addictive. I would struggle with this for years to come. Even though I eventually sought help, once a person develops an eating disorder or any other type of addiction, it is something he or she must live with for the rest of his or her life. I have learned to shift my focus so that I don't fall back into that deadly trap.

Despite my crippling eating disorder, I continued to earn good grades, but I always focused on what was still to come. Earning an A in one class meant I had to earn A's in all of my other classes. I was very hard on myself if I fell behind the slightest bit, even if it was in a class that wasn't related to engineering. Rather than always being consumed with what was next, I wish I had seen the progress I was making and enjoyed my accomplishments as I earned them.

☑ Follow your interests

Along our paths of earning degrees in STEM disciplines, we will have opportunities to choose classes that best match our interests. At some point, we will be asked to decide on an area of emphasis that can help get us into the specific profession or industry we wish to work in after graduation. By doing ample research, we can decide how to narrow our individual areas of focus.

Oftentimes we can only home in on what we *want* to do by identifying what we *don't want* to do. On paper, mechanical engineering appealed to me. I was intrigued with what mechanical engineers actually *did* all day. One of the classes that my university required for their mechanical program, but not for their electrical program, was dynamics. This at first sounded interesting. Almost immediately, however, I realized that the kinematics of a particle and mechanical vibrations did not interest me. After just two weeks, it was clear that the mechanical track was not for me. Even though the semester had started, my professor allowed me to switch to electrical engineering. I was thankful that my wrong decision did not delay my schooling, but even if it had, it would have been worth it just to come to the realization that I truly wanted to be an electrical engineer.

There is something mysterious about currents. With civil and mechanical engineering, what you see is what you get, for the most part, and that is part of the appeal to some people. For me, though, I liked the idea of working with something you cannot see. At the time, I viewed currents as somewhat romantic, somewhat dangerous, and I still do. Finding the right specialty to focus on in my studies reinforced that I was heading in the right direction and encouraged me to push forward. Typically all engineering majors—whether mechanical, electrical, or civil—will take the same classes freshman year and the first semester of their sophomore year. These entry-level classes give a foundation for all engineering specialties while also providing some exposure to the different disciplines. This is the time to really think about your interest and talk with professors about future classes.

Susan Fitzpatrick, president of the Association for Women in Science and vice president of the James S. McDonnell Foundation, trained in biochemistry and biophysics in the late '70s and early '80s. "This was a time when those fields were fairly representative of gender imbalance," she said. "Often, I was the only woman in the lab, or one of only a handful of women in a whole department. As an undergraduate, I was a biology major, but I really loved my chemistry classes, which was how I ended up going into biochemistry."

Susan remembers being the first person in anyone's memory to score straight 100s on her exams in physical chemistry. "It's the course that everyone dreads taking because it's so hard. And yet no one ever, ever mentioned to me that I might consider becoming a chemist. Never. And it didn't occur to me either, even though I was excelling in this type of coursework and really enjoyed it. The prevailing attitude just seemed to be that 'girls' didn't do chemistry. I guarantee if I'd been a male majoring in some other field, the chemistry department would have tried to pull me in."

In retrospect, Susan realizes that this didn't shock her. "It all seems strange, but at the time, it didn't. I enjoyed it so much that it was internally rewarding. I wasn't aware of missing any particular opportunities, because there were so many interesting areas that you could study, regardless of what type of science you ultimately entered. If you can find that internal reward—if you love learning, testing yourself, designing experiments, and so forth—you almost don't notice things, such as gender imbalance, going on around you."

College is an optimal time to explore what truly interests you. You no doubt have ideas about what you want to do, but those ideas will really only be well defined once you investigate and experience different options. If you find yourself on a path that fails to hold your interest, it is never too late to explore other options. Though no one ever told me that, I am telling you now because of my good fortune in making the right decision.

CONCLUSION

While compiling material for this chapter, I talked with a colleague of mine who recently graduated with a master's degree in engineering. She started her bachelor's degree with about 150 students, only ten of whom were female. Before the end of the first semester, half of the females had changed their major (in the end, my colleague was the only one of the remaining five to go on to complete her bachelor's degree in five years). While the gender imbalance presented her with the expected reactions from her male classmates, it was the words of her electrical engineering professor that stood out the most in her memory. During class one day, he blatantly told the forty students, "Women should only be allowed in school to teach men English and history." She remembers this statement word-for-word and told me she and one of the other females in the class were so taken aback that they filed a formal complaint to the administrators of the electrical engineering program.

She also had a story about the more subtle biased assumptions that continue to riddle STEM disciplines. About midway through earning her bachelor's degree, she was part of a design class that required students to build a mechanical device. In order to use the school's machine shop, students had to fill out and pass a take-home safety quiz. One morning a male student accompanied her to the basement of the engineering building to procure two copies of the safety quiz from the machine shop. The machinist who oversaw the shop greeted them, and they each asked for the quiz. In response, the machinist retrieved one safety quiz and handed it to her male friend. My colleague had to explain that she was an engineering student and would also need a copy of the safety quiz. It might not seem like much, but as any female student can attest to, comments and actions such as those demonstrated by the machinist build up and require energy to overcome.

The last story she shared with me took place when she neared the completion of her bachelor's degree. Upon hearing that she had been accepted to the graduate school's master's degree program, a number of her peers started rumors about how she qualified to get in—questioning which professors she had to sleep with to advance. These peers, who by coincidence were struggling to pass their undergrad classes, had been with her in the same study groups and were counted among her closest friends.

Stories such as these reveal all too clearly that gender bias still remains in STEM programs at the college level. Sometimes overt and sometimes subtle, behaviors and comments exhibited by the opposite sex can be taxing on young female students. But attempting to work with male students instead of avoiding them, recognizing our accomplishments, and following our interests can help us push through the bias and continue toward the goal of graduating.

For inspiration, tools, and resources, visit www.UnlockingYourBrilliance.com and www.STEMspire.org.

Chapter 3

FIND THE RIGHT CAREER PATH

As my junior year ended and the *real world* beyond graduation drew closer, I still was unsure which arena of electrical engineering I wanted to work within. So, the summer before my senior year I took an internship with an electric-chip manufacturer in Harrisburg. I worked a 9-to-5 job in an office environment and was responsible for certain parameters in developing a technical computer program. I came to dread the endless deskwork, but I quickly came to enjoy my coworkers.

Internships are a great way to experience the work environment and explore different options within your discipline of study. Internships provide fantastic on-the-job training and often lead to job offers after graduation.

The area of private engineering is not one that a lot of electrical engineers necessarily explore upon graduation. Because of this, I believe that my school did an inadequate job explaining all of the options engineering students have after they graduate. As a freshman I was exposed to some of the different options, but I was eighteen years old. Since I still had such a long way to go, I did not see the urgency of selecting a detailed career path. I have since heard this criticism from other engineers, and I believe it is an area in which institutions of higher learning could improve. If engineering program faculty members informed students of all their available options, the students would be better prepared to establish and work toward their career goals. I understand that some of the responsibility is on the students themselves, but it is difficult for young adults to make life decisions if they are unclear about their options. However, now that we are deeply embedded in an information age, students carry more responsibility for researching the areas they wish to pursue.

THE HURDLE: CONFRONTING DISSATISFACTION WITH WORK

Women who choose to follow careers in STEM disciplines face unique and frustrating challenges. Even after we establish ourselves in our careers, we continue to encounter potential career-ending traps. Not only do women in STEM careers have higher attrition rates than do their male counterparts—especially within the first ten years on the job—we also have higher attrition rates than women in other careers. The general belief that men outperform women in math and science fields is one of the reasons for the high attrition rate. Other reasons include cognitive gender differences, a woman's lack of interest in the STEM fields, work-life balance issues, and bias (Hewlett, 2008). This is an important subject to acknowledge and correct; otherwise, we will never level the playing field. This chapter focuses on overcoming the obstacles that can drive us to be dissatisfied with our work and potentially end the careers we worked so hard to attain.

In the STEM fields, conquering post-secondary education is vastly different than conquering a career. College and university programs teach guidelines, problem solving, and time management. Higher education is the traditional route the majority of us take when attempting to find careers that will allow us to live comfortably. However, undergraduate studies do not always prepare us for the working world and are not always the best indicator for how well we will do once we land jobs in certain fields. It is not until we join the workforce that the pressure is on us to truly apply our knowledge. The pressures facing young females entering the STEM workforce are humbling and extremely trying. Without much warning, these pressures can lead to high levels of dissatisfaction.

The responsibility we have in academic programs pales in comparison to the responsibility we will have in the working world, especially in STEM fields. In both arenas (school and work), we are assigned tasks and asked to complete them to the best of our abilities. In school, if we do as our instructors request, we get a decent grade; if we don't, we get a less-than-decent grade. When we start our careers, we are being paid to achieve results. Multimillion-dollar projects can ultimately fail because of our workmanship. Plus, in most STEM occupations, our work can impact the safety of others.

STRATEGIES FOR MAKING IT THROUGH

Like the majority of my classmates, I had it ingrained in my head that, just as college seemed to be the right thing to do after high school, working for a big corporation seemed to make sense after college. Big firms that focused on electronics-based engineering were soaking up most of my classmates. At the time, those jobs were prevalent and were the ones we were most exposed to in college. However, those were not the only jobs that our engineering degrees qualified us for.

So what's a girl to do? The following are some tips for empowering yourself regardless of the level of information or exposure that's readily available.

⊘ Know what's out there

As we approach graduation day, we must take responsibility for finding out all the types of work we are qualified for. No one else is going to do it for us.

During my senior year, numerous engineering firms were interested in hiring students fresh out of college. But engineering job availability, just like job availability in nearly every industry, is cyclical. Because I did not know any better, I thought I wanted to be in research and development, which fell in line with my internship experience. Throughout the first semester of my senior year, I spent my time going to job fairs and interviewing with different firms that offered R&D positions.

Also at one point in my senior year, I purchased a book that listed the major engineering firms in the United States and throughout the world. I looked through the book and picked out a number of firms I thought I would like to work for. After doing more research, I narrowed down the list. As graduation approached, however, I still was not sure what it was that I wanted to do. This was one major area in which I felt that my schooling had not prepared me. I was exposed to some of the different engineering careers available to someone with a degree, but I was not instructed on how to go about the pursuit. I thought I knew so much coming out of college, but there was an entire world of engineering I had barely been exposed to.

By the spring semester of my senior year, I had lined up an entry-level job with an engineering consulting firm based in Arlington, Virginia, that worked closely with the US Air Force. The firm flew me down for an all-day interview and showed me their facilities, which were close to the Pentagon. I was a senior in college, eager to be pursuing a job in the field in which I was earning my degree. I decided to accept their offer because it sounded like exciting work that was in line with my degree, or so I thought at the time. Also at this time, I was starting to get back together with my high school boyfriend. We had been in touch with each other again and the romance started to bloom. I did date other men on and off in college, but the relationship with my high school boyfriend just felt right. Stay tuned—the story continues.

None of the obstacles I encountered in school ever had me running back home to Harrisburg fearing I had made a horrible mistake in my choice of studies or career. Once I started my first job in the real world, though, I soon realized that I needed an advisor even more in the workforce than I did during college.

⊘ Seek out internships

Seeking out various internships in college is a way to become exposed to all of the behind-the-scenes happenings that we cannot learn in a classroom. Being involved with an operating company allows us to see how people work as a team, how they overcome challenges, and how the team is managed. Every firm is different, and by seeking out internships, we give ourselves the opportunity to understand what kinds of bosses and teams we like working with.

Also, in a competitive job market, many potential employers are going to accept applications only from candidates who can demonstrate they have a degree *and* real-world experience; seeking out an internship is one way of proving the latter. When applying for our first internships, most of us will likely not have any work experience to pull from and outline on our résumés. Don't let this prevent you from creating an entry-level résumé that includes your course loads during your last two years of study, the anticipated date of graduation, related workshops you have attended, community involvement, and related interests. Look for places to submit your résumé: at job fairs, related associations, and university career-placement programs. Also, you can contact firms directly to inquire about internship opportunities.

If for some reason an official internship program doesn't work out or isn't the right fit, find other avenues to learn everything you can about your field. For Lori Polasek, marine mammal biologist and professor at University of Alaska-Fairbanks, dissecting a frog during a required biology class her sophomore year in college was a revelatory experience. "I'd found something I could really be passionate about," she said. "Once I chose my new direction, I jumped in hard and fast, because I was now two years behind other students in the field."

Lori sought out biology teachers, volunteering to do "anything needed" in their labs. "I stayed at school over the summers to take classes and volunteer on field projects. I picked up odd jobs in labs. I quickly gained experience and exposure to lab techniques, fieldwork, and faculty that I would not have encountered otherwise."

By the time Lori graduated with a bachelor's degree, she had gained more experience than some graduate students. "This facilitated my entry into graduate school," she explained, "to eventually obtain my PhD. This all began with a family that never limited my possibilities, which made the transition to a new field quick and easy. But it would not have been possible without stepping outside of the classroom to gain additional experience."

Today, Lori receives dozens of applications each year from potential graduate students. "They all look similar on paper," she observed. "They all have good grades and positive references, but the one thing that makes them stand out above the rest is experience outside the classroom."

⊘ Work toward your working goals

Rarely does anyone exit college and immediately work at the job of their dreams. Dissatisfaction with our entry-level jobs, at least on some level, is normal.

After we complete college and go on to secure jobs in STEM disciplines, we oftentimes find ourselves ill-prepared for the abrasive work environments. As I mentioned earlier in this chapter, far more women than men leave their STEM careers. For instance, in 2006 the Society of Women Engineers (SWE) released a retention study of more than six thousand individuals who received their engineering degrees between 1985 and 2003. At the time of the survey, one in four female respondents was either unemployed or not employed in engineering or a related field. At the same time, only one in ten male respondents was not in the engineering field (Society of Women Engineers, 2006). This means women were either not being hired into engineering positions or they were leaving them shortly after entering into the STEM workforce.

According to a report published in 2011 by the US Economics and Statistics Administration, "Women with a STEM degree are less likely than their male counterparts to work in a STEM occupation . . . About 40 percent (2.7 million) of men with STEM college degrees work in STEM jobs, whereas only 26 percent (0.6 million) of women with STEM degrees work in STEM jobs" (US Economics and Statistics Administration, 2011).

For whatever number of different reasons, we do know that women are leaving STEM careers at much higher rates than men. "Hostile work environments and extreme job pressures" are the main reasons for attrition. Other reasons include a male-dominated environment that does not cater to the needs of women—especially those with families—and the lack of flex time (Hewlett, 2008).

For us, while the gender differences in school may have been apparent, all students still shared the common goal of securing a degree. Once we enter the workforce, we will likely encounter work environments that are dominated by men of various levels of seniority. The bias against females in STEM careers shared among men of our same age may be subtle, but the bias shared among much older men can be more overt. Plus, we may find that we are entering into an environment in which there's a tight work-group of men who have handled projects together for a number of years. This can be extremely intimidating for a young woman with no real-world work experience. When I first moved to Reno to start PK Electrical, I was a stranger in a new land, and to make matters worse, I was a woman in a very male-dominated profession. Clients were reluctant to try us because we were new and not part of the typically male group that was known around town. It took perseverance and determination on my part to get through that challenging time. I relied heavily on my personal and family support for encouragement. Observing and learning from other engineers (mainly men) in the work environment also helped. I kept a positive attitude because I knew I was not going to let the obstacles stop me. It was a difficult couple of years.

While we were in college we likely strengthened our backbones and learned to deal with challenges creatively and satisfactorily, but this does not mean we have to put up with *everything*. If the job market is weak, we will think harder about leaving a job that allows us to pay our bills yet tests our patience. Whatever the economy, however, we will likely have to make difficult decisions, learn to adapt, and do things we do not want to do while searching for the STEM career we have always dreamed of. Sometimes you need to stay with an unsatisfactory job just to support yourself.

My job with the engineering consulting firm was in Arlington, Virginia, which was about a 120-mile drive south of my hometown. For the very first time, I was living on my own and responsible for my own well-being. I had to budget my time and money, build new friendships, and start a new job where the expectations weren't quite clear. I was doing R&D for aircraft aviation systems to determine their efficiency. While it sounded interesting on paper, it was rigorous, it was tedious, and it was awful. I hated it. There was no application of what I had learned at Widener, and

I had no sense of accomplishment. I was not using any math *or* any science—the two cornerstone subjects I had arduously studied for four years. Instead of being out in the field or on a job site, I was stuck behind a desk reading at tremendous length about aviation systems. After stepping up to the challenges of working in a male-dominated field, I was behind the scenes in the presence of no one, male or female. I did not know what to do. Looking back, I should have taken advantage of the HR department to express my discontent with my job. I was shy, young, and unclear about my options. I strongly recommend that you seek the attention of supervisors, advisors, or the HR department when you are experiencing job dissatisfaction. There may be opportunities available within the company that you are not aware of.

The boredom of not using any of the skills I had worked so hard to develop had me occasionally going home on weekends in tears. I felt my life was a mess. I dreaded going to work at a job I hated, and I constantly thought, "Is this it?"

On top of my growing frustration with the type of work I was performing was the unease I felt within the environment and culture of a big corporation. Fearing that I would be caught in dry R&D jobs for the rest of my life, I was back to looking for new work within months. Looking back, I probably shouldn't have jumped on the first exciting job offer that came my way. I recommend spending quality time learning about the company you are about to work for. I also encourage writing down a set of clearly defined expectations and goals. Throughout your career, always work toward your working goals.

I was so unhappy with my job, but I was also unhappy because my high school sweetheart, the man I had fallen in love with, was stationed in Las Vegas, Nevada, at Nellis Air Force Base. My job and responsibilities were in Virginia, but my heart was in Las Vegas with him. Occasionally I was able to visit him there, and on one such trip, we became engaged. Now I really didn't want to be at a job I dreaded!

⊘ Practice self-analysis continually

The first handful of jobs we take out of college teach us an extraordinary amount about what we really want from our work product and the workplace. In college we might think that money is the most important thing to consider when weighing job possibilities. After working jobs with great pay but extremely long hours, we may find that freedom is more important than money. The essential thing to remember is that we won't know until we try. We have to remain flexible and not be afraid to leave one job for another just because of the possibility of an uncomfortable transition.

Going through a process of real self-analysis and asking ourselves questions—What is it we love to do? What type of work do we really enjoy? How can we feel fulfilled by our work? What types of challenges do we enjoy? What are we most passionate about within our fields? And so on—can help us make difficult decisions when we come to career roadblocks. If we don't like what we're doing and we've given it our best shot, we should take time to become very clear about what it is that we don't like about our current position. From there we have to decide if it is best for us to move on. We can't be afraid to change jobs, particularly early in our careers; it's important to get on the right track. There is an abundance of information on this subject to help you make the decision that is best for you. Tom Rath's bestselling *Strengths-Finder 2.0* is a tremendous resource I highly recommend.

I was becoming more and more dissatisfied with the work I was doing in Virginia, and my fiancé was working as a combat arms instructor in Nevada. Originally, he had planned on moving back to the East Coast as soon as the opportunity arose. However, I began to consider the possibility of moving his direction. While on a brief trip to visit him, I riffled through a phone book and ripped out a handful of pages that listed engineering companies.

When I returned to the East Coast, I began calling every firm listed on the hijacked yellow pages, without really knowing exactly what each one did. When I happened to call TJ Krob, a private engineering firm, I found out they were hiring, and they requested that I send along my résumé. From there, the next steps moved pretty quickly; it was equal parts exciting and terrifying. I flew out the next week for an interview and they offered me a job on the spot. Thankfully, engineers were in need all over the country at the time, which made my overt job trading a bit easier.

Luckily, I had stumbled upon just what I was looking for. Most electrical engineers currently follow careers within the area of communications/electronics. Only around 5 percent of us go into the kind of work that TJ Krob handled, which is working on building systems (lighting, power distribution, fire alarm), as opposed to the work of an electronics-based company that produces electronic chips.

When I initially met with Tom Krob, the owner of the firm, he explained what the business did; I was interested (and relieved) because we would be doing calculations and true application. It was perfect. (I would later realize it was also perfect because Tom Krob would become one of the most influential men in my life.)

In February of 1990, after only eight months in Northern Virginia, I made plans to move across the country to join Tom Krob's much smaller, private engineering firm. What I knew about Nevada was limited at best. In fact, during my exit interview, when the woman in human resources told me she was from Reno, I remember smiling and thinking she was talking about a suburb of Las Vegas, not a mountainous city eight hours to the north! Obviously my geographical knowledge of the western United States was not up to par; how could you drive eight hours and still be in the same state?

Regardless, my bags were packed and off I drove with my dad to a part of the country that was foreign to me. The people were nicer (helpful even), the weather was warmer, the sun came out more often, and the landscape was blanketed with desert. I was thrilled to finally be near my fiancé. Before I had much time to explore or become familiar with the area, I was in the office of TJ Krob to complete the hiring process. It was really the first time I was able to ask in-depth questions and get a better idea of what it was that the firm did and what my responsibilities would be. I guess I had developed the dangerous tendency of taking a job *first* and figuring out what I would be doing *second*. Thankfully, I was still somewhat fresh out of college and had the flexibility to explore a variety of jobs. Without doing so, I wouldn't be in the career I love today.

Finding the new job gave me a sense of relief and satisfaction. After being hired at TJ Krob, I eventually quit questioning every-thing—*Had I made a huge mistake with engineering? Is this what I really wanted? Am I going to be stuck in jobs I hate forever?* My new job reinforced that I did have control over where I worked and for whom. I was also pleased with my salary. Typically, women earn approximately 20 percent less than their male counterparts. Although I never felt that I was earning less than a male in my same position, this unacceptable gender imbalance does exist. I would recommend researching appropriate salaries and standing up for what you believe that you deserve. In my business practice, I never pay a woman a lesser salary simply because she is a woman. Salaries in my company are based on experience and position, never gender.

For Ruth Charney, president-elect of the Association for Women in Mathematics and professor at Brandeis University, gender imbalance in her field has been a motivating factor, and understanding the value she places on improving equality has helped her through some big career decisions. "The chair of my department at Ohio State University fell ill and I agreed to take over as interim chair for one year," she explained. "I found the job quite rewarding, and I was asked to stay on for a full four-year term. But given the size of the department and the scope of the job, I knew I could not maintain a serious research program while serving as chair. An important factor in my decision was my conviction that for women to be taken seriously in mathematics, we needed more women researchers, not more women administrators. I declined, and returned to my research."

⊘ Find a mentor to help you navigate the way

The value of mentorship is a recurring theme in this book, and for good reason. Not only can having a mentor make our transitions into our new positions smoother, but also mentors can be long-lasting resources of information. Finding a mentor early on can do wonders for the amount of satisfaction we find in our jobs.

The process of choosing a mentor differs depending on the occupation, the culture of the company, and the availability of our superiors. Most workplace environments encourage mentor-protégé relationships. They develop naturally in the workplace where both parties see each other frequently and comfortably.

It should go without saying, but oftentimes men make for extraordinary mentors. As female scientists, engineers, or mathematicians, we cannot limit our searches for mentors strictly to females because we want to become female managers, chairpersons, business owners, and so on. We should begin to seek advice from those holding the positions we hope to fill one day, regardless of the position holder's gender.

Instead of presenting ourselves as desperate or helpless, we can approach potential mentors with confidence and interest. While it is not commonplace to ask someone flat out to be a mentor, we can initiate a potential mentor-mentee relationship by expressing our gratitude for someone's advice and making it clear that we hope he or she will continue offering it. We should remember to ask questions, seek the individual's advice, and take an interest in his or her work—but also know when to get out of the way.

The people we choose as mentors need to have the capacity and capability to lead us toward success. However, our mentors may not always be the people with whom we get along best or those who are our immediate superiors. A mentor is not only someone who is willing to take the time to teach us techniques and processes but also someone who takes an interest in our long-term advancement. Because this person can see our potential, he or she is willing to go beyond job duties and put in the extra work to ensure that we gain the understanding needed to progress.

That said, we also need to ensure that we get what we need out of mentoring relationships. Madhu Lal-Nag, a scientist with the National Institutes of Health and president-elect of a chapter of Graduate Women in Science, ran into a hurdle with one of her early mentor relationships. Madhu says she's been fortunate to have mostly worked in "stimulating and innovative work environments," with one exception that occurred during her time as a young post-baccalaureate scientist.

"I had the opportunity to work with a very demanding mentor, who happened to be a woman scientist trying hard to make it in a predominantly male institute," Madhu explained. "She was exceptionally bright and often impatient with her employees, quick with the admonition and scanty with praise. My faith in my choice of career was severely tested. I began to question my aptitude and ability for science, because constantly being told by a senior scientist that I was doing everything wrong had me believing that I truly was not meant to be a scientist."

Finally, Madhu discussed the situation with another lab assistant and realized that the problem wasn't in her abilities. "It was impossible that everybody who worked for her was inept," she said. The outcome of that revelation was life changing. "I stuck to my guns and stayed in science, despite the situation I was in. I found a new mentor. If I had to do anything differently, I would have found another mentor much sooner, instead of being plagued by self-doubt."

Madhu's advice for young women in similar situations? "Always trust your gut instinct," she said, "and stick to your guns. Speak out and find yourself a mentor. We are in science to learn, and constructive criticism is part and parcel of the scientific process.

However, when that criticism turns personal, is unwarranted, and has nothing to do with science, stand up for yourself."

Although not everybody is cut out to play a mentoring role, many professionals will take on the opportunity to be a mentor if we show our appreciation for their efforts. We, too, have to put in the extra work in order to demonstrate that their guidance is leading to on-the-job results. We must prove to them that we're taking their efforts seriously by showing them we understand and are implementing their expertise. While the feeling of making a difference in our careers (and lives) will be a rewarding payoff for mentors, these professionals will inevitably want to see us reach professional goals and milestones.

Mentors have a wealth of knowledge, and having access to that knowledge can greatly trim our learning curves. Another advantage to finding a quality mentor early on in any given job is the mentor's ability to thwart discrimination. Learning the correct protocol from a superior will help prove to our peers that we are capable. Being the new person in a company with a tight-knit group of employees can be trying for anyone. And, for a woman entering a good-ol'-boy workforce, it can be extremely intimidating. Pairing with a mentor will not only link us to someone with seniority, it will also help us carry out operations the way the company's team prefers. A mentor will help us avoid costly (read: embarrassing) mistakes commonly made by new employees.

Because of both the career and the mentor relationship I was about to start, the day I met Tom Krob would become one of the most fortunate days in my career. I had the foundation that I learned in school, but the experience Tom provided taught me nearly everything I know today about being successful in the field of engineering (and business). Because the firm was small, I was able to spend quality time with Tom; I was allowed to really observe him and learn from his actions. He showed me the business side of engineering, which was something I was not exposed to in school. I worked closely with him for a number of years and soaked up everything he taught me, something that was not encouraged in the environment of a large corporate company. In transferring to TJ Krob in Nevada, I found my home as an electrical engineer.

CONCLUSION

Our interests in a STEM field may have gotten us through the course material in college, but that does not guarantee we will fall in love with our first related jobs. There are too many variables to account for when trying to select the best job to take. Plus, our preferences change. Dissatisfaction with our jobs is normal and has to be dealt with. The worst thing we can do is ignore the pressing issues and hope they will go away; they rarely ever just disappear. We have to be proactive, and sometimes that means leaving one job for another. Along your journey, remember the strategies discussed in this chapter. Your dream job is out there and—just like anything worth obtaining—you have to be patient and committed to finding it.

 For inspiration, tools, and resources, visit www.UnlockingYourBrilliance.com and www.STEMspire.org.

Chapter 4

DO THE WORK WELL AND
RESPECT WILL FOLLOW

At last I had found an environment within which I was applying my skills and gaining real-world experience at a dizzying pace. I enjoyed working, but I was surprised that I continued to be challenged by some of the same biases I had encountered in college from my male classmates. I was taking on more responsibility at TJ Krob, but my male counterparts were not showing the level of respect I believed I was earning as a capable electrical engineer. They would second-guess my recommendations and opinions and ask another male for his opinion instead.

Challenges by no means disappear just because we find a STEM career that is the right fit for us. Once we find our places, we again have to accept that we will most likely be surrounded by men, and the skepticism or prejudice some of them still harbor toward women in math and science will affect our workdays. Those attitudes will feel even more frustrating because, having battled them for four or five years at the university level, we must persist in the fight to prove that we belong in our fields.

In my situation, even as Tom Krob began to assign me additional responsibilities, I remember coming back from countless meetings in which people assumed I was his secretary or personal assistant, not one of the company's lead engineers. Of course it was aggravating; I had worked tirelessly to secure my place within a reputable engineering firm (and moved across the country to do so). But now, as I look back, I think the reactions I was garnering from others had as much to do with my behavior as it did my gender. In the strategies section that follows, I'll pinpoint what those behaviors were and offer you practical suggestions for how to avoid them in your own work environment.

THE HURDLE: EARNING THE RESPECT OF OUR MALE COLLEAGUES

Gender bias still remains in the STEM fields: some of it is explicit, most of it implicit. And sometimes other females demonstrate the same bias that male colleagues do. As I will discuss in this chapter, we cannot allow every raised eyebrow or belittling comment to whittle away at our confidence or send us into a fit of anger or despair. Although we may remember the demeaning comments for years to come, we have to learn to shake them off and remain confident in our abilities.

As females with advanced positions in a male-dominated industry, we must focus on building relationships with our coworkers and developing support for our ideas. You will encounter male employees—whether in positions above or below you—who are not comfortable working with women. Whatever their reason, you cannot afford to become consumed in trying to convince them their bias is unwarranted. Simply do your job to the best of your abilities and allow your actions to argue your point.

As I was collecting research for this book, many sister engineers openly shared with me their stories of the gender bias they continue to encounter. Some of them have been in the field for thirty years and some are not yet through their first year. Regardless of how long they've been working, they all had similar stories of gender bias.

Cindy, who is a civil engineer, took a job with a very conservative firm in Virginia early in her career. The few female employees were encouraged to dress "conservatively," which meant "in a dress." Even when visiting job sites, the women would wear dresses along with their bulky work boots. Cindy remembers arriving on a particular project site in North Carolina with her coworker, the firm's senior engineer (another female). Upon their arrival, the area's public works director greeted them. During introductions, Cindy remembers him saying, "Wow, look at that; two lady engineers."

At another time later in her career, she was working with a Nevada firm and visiting a job site in the eastern part of the state. She had been warned by other coworkers that she needed to "really know her stuff" because the contractors in that region would try and "put her in her place." Cindy said the contractors in eastern Nevada would tell her "not to worry her pretty little head" about certain aspects of the projects. Even though they would call her "sweetie," "darling," and "honey," Cindy noticed that she could always earn their respect by coming across as knowledgeable about the different jobs her firm was performing.

My colleagues shared with me numerous stories of being mistaken at meetings for secretaries or assistants or as the boss's wife at a company party. Cindy told me a female secretary at one firm mistook her for a secretary and asked how long she'd been in the position. Cindy politely said she was an engineer, and the secretary's eyes lit up as she said, "You're an engineer? Imagine that." Cindy joked that she thought about saying, "Yep, and I can vote too," but she held her tongue.

I applaud Cindy's security in who she is as a woman and competent engineer, which frees her to tease, joke, and laugh off the narrow-minded thinking of others. More power to her!

STRATEGIES FOR MAKING IT THROUGH

As females in male-dominated industries, we have to work harder to earn respect, and it all starts with our behaviors and how we carry and present ourselves. Males can walk onto a job site, into a lab, or into a meeting and immediately have others attribute to them some level of credibility simply because they are male; we don't have that luxury. So what's a girl to do? The following strategies are important for all women who wish to earn respect as they earn more responsibility in their careers.

⊘Be heard

When others would assume I was Tom's assistant, I believe it had a lot to do with my hesitancy to speak up, especially at project meetings. I had grown more assertive by my senior year in college, but I found myself reverting to being hesitant because I was in a new workplace and was new to the level of leadership with which I had been entrusted.

Oftentimes, soft-spoken women are swallowed up in a meeting room filled with boisterous men. I was no exception. When I was surrounded at project meetings by men with type-A personalities, they were, by nature, very dominating, which made voicing my opinions a real struggle for me. The men were allowed to be themselves; their voices carried, and they could comfortably communicate without changing their inherent behavior. I, on the other hand, was forced to change my communication behavior in order to be heard. This became even more necessary when I was put in charge of controlling certain situations. I realized that I had to speak up to be heard. I had to talk louder and not be afraid to jump into a conversation. At times, when there are a bunch of loud men in a room, it's hard to get a word in edgewise. I think taking on new challenges outside of your comfort zone can help you overcome this and other obstacles. Even recently, by taking on the challenge of becoming the president of the Reno/Tahoe chapter of the Entrepreneurs' Organization (EO), I knew I would gain an opportunity to improve my speaking and interaction skills with men. My EO forum mates have noticed a huge improvement in both areas since my presidency. It is a continuous learning process.

Women who are strong communicators don't have to behave differently in the workplace. Because they have mastered communication skills in one-on-one and group settings, these women can behave just as they would in any other environment, regardless of the fact that they are in the minority. For women like me, who are more reserved and tend to withhold their opinions, they must find resources to improve their communication skills, particularly if they strive to be in leadership positions.

Madhu Lal-Nag works for the National Institutes of Health and is the president-elect of a chapter of Graduate Women in Science. Evolution, she believes, plays a large part in the situation women scientists find themselves in today. "We're wading the waters of a predominantly male terrain," she observes, "fighting for a stronghold. We find ourselves fighting fire with fire, becoming 'male-like' in order to compete with men. This is our only and biggest mistake. In order to compete in a predominantly male arena, we must excel as women to achieve mutual understanding—and to earn anyone's respect, male or female."

Early in her scientific career, Madhu says she spent a lot of time doing what she was told to do, "in order to earn the respect of my male colleagues. A well-meaning male mentor finally told me that if I wanted to stand out in my field of research, I would first have to overcome the initial 'stage fright' that took hold of me every time I voiced an opinion."

So Madhu found her inner strength. "I worked hard to ignore the hammering of my heart as I spoke at scientific conferences to a variety of audiences," she says, "because the need for people to respect my science was greater than any fear I had of not being respected by my male colleagues. To my greatest surprise, the more I spoke of my science, the more confident I became, and the respect accorded to me as a scientist was automatic."

There are a lot of ways to improve your communication skills. For example, Toastmasters is a great organization to help you improve your public speaking abilities. Joining and becoming active in a local professional or community organization is another way. Sitting on a board forces you to interact with board members and talk publicly—at least in front of them. I have found this to be a tremendous help. One of the first boards I was part of was the local Society of Women Engineers (SWE) professional chapter. It gave me an opportunity to not only meet other people but also to express my opinion in front of others in a safe environment. I have also been asked to teach a college class for one day, explaining to students just what, exactly, an electrical engineer does. Take advantage of every opportunity you are given.

Some women may have internalized the view from an earlier era that it is out of place for them to be opinionated in a room filled with men. Such women may have to break out of their comfort zones, however, in order to be effective as team members or leaders. Because men dominate certain fields, they also control the communication environments in those fields. Men have had primary influence over what is perceived as effective communication in most STEM disciplines and industries, and that will not change solely because of a woman's presence. The communication context has been established in order to help men thrive. While women may feel out of place, we must adapt. It may be uncomfortable at first, but it gets easier.

I remember one of my first project meetings at TJ Krob. It was at an architect's office, and there were probably ten to twelve people in the room. I was so intimidated by the others that I don't think I said two words. I remember thinking, *What if I say something stupid and I get laughed at?* As the project progressed, I became more comfortable with the people on the team and eventually was able to speak with ease at the team meetings. Now I don't think anything of it. It is all a matter of practice: the more you do it, the more you develop a comfort level. I have a staff of eighteen that I have to speak in front of every Monday at our staff meetings. Each speaking opportunity is a learning experience. Take every opportunity to learn and grow.

In the course of gathering information in order to make informed decisions, women naturally and automatically ask a lot of questions. As a minority in the typically male-dominated STEM fields, however, we can often feel that we will be judged as incompetent if we ask questions. We cannot let our gender get in the way of acquiring the knowledge we need to successfully do our jobs. As women in professional positions, we are overly aware when men outnumber us in our fields of work. This may make us feel as if we are constantly being scrutinized and evaluated, but this cannot force us to behave in ways that are counterproductive. By asking men questions, we are not putting them in a higher position. If, by title, they are in a higher position, then part of their job is to help their colleagues understand how to do their jobs better. If we do not know something, or we need clarification, we cannot be afraid to ask questions.

Being a woman who works in a male-dominated field is "an astonishing advantage," according to Mary Fernandez, board chairman of MentorNet and assistant vice president of research at AT&T Labs. "I have never felt that it was, in fact, a disadvantage. When I talk to young women who are entering the computer science field, I remind them that their voice sounds different when they speak in a group of men, and this difference is a distinct advantage."

Mary acknowledged the research that says women aren't being heard in male-dominated environments, but stated, "The truth is, a woman who works in a male-dominated field brings a different dynamic to every group. I've found this to be an incredible advantage in every technical and business situation that I've been in." She offered an example from a recent conflict in her work life.

"I was confronted by a much more senior person in my organization who was giving me a hard time about a fairly big technical problem. I got up close to him, looked him in the eye, and said, 'I want to understand why you're so upset. I respect your knowledge and expertise, and I need you to be a team player on this. I'm here to listen to you.' And then I shut up."

Mary said she thinks her approach disarmed him. "Often when there's confrontation among males, there can be a little one-upmanship," she explained. "Instead, I used the approach of recognizing that the other person knew something that I didn't know, and then I said that aloud."

As women, Mary added, "we are trained by society to listen. And if you listen sincerely, really hearing the other person and echoing back to him what he said, it can diffuse tense situations and bring people toward consensus much faster. I've been pretty successful at doing that through the years, and I do attribute that to the female dynamic. Genuinely being open to learning from others really levels the playing field."

☑ Produce accurate results

Ruzena Bajcsy, professor of electrical engineering and computer sciences at University of California at Berkeley, says she has managed to earn the respect of male colleagues through the years by producing results. "You can't just talk; you have to show what you can do. I'm an engineer, I have designed things, and I have demonstrated new ideas."

Academia, Ruzena feels, "is traditionally very conservative. When you come up with a new idea, people tend to be skeptical—they want you to show them how it works, and what it really means. So I had to build my own systems, and over the course of three years, I developed a special kind of camera. I was able to show everyone that it worked, which made it difficult to debate. Producing results is the only way I know of to satisfy the skeptics."

Ruzena also described how producing results combats a subtle bias she sees in the STEM fields: "There is a general idea that women are not as tough or as persistent as men. But I think things are improving because there are now more of us—and more of us who are delivering. I think things are changing for the better for women in engineering. You have to believe in yourself; it's as simple as that."

I have always been self-conscious about giving the correct information when someone asks me a question. Early in my career, I was never afraid to tell anyone that I wanted to check with Tom before giving him or her a definitive answer. To me, my behavior resulted from the high value I put on providing accurate information, but I can now see how others could interpret it as my lacking confidence in myself as an engineer. Certain others may have seen this behavior as my inability to do anything without Tom's permission.

Sometimes we may want to protect our image and confidence by spitting out the answers to questions right when they are posed, even if the information we have is not complete. In my experience, men are more apt to give information on the spot, whereas women are more likely to make sure their information is accurate before they offer it. Both men and women, though, can be guilty of giving inaccurate information for the perceived benefit of appearing credible. It is perfectly fine, however, to sacrifice the appearance of confident expertise in order to supply an answer that is accurate and complete. In the long run, giving *accurate* answers will do more to boost our professional credibility than giving *quick* answers. No pride is lost in telling someone you will do the proper research and get back to them with an *accurate* answer shortly.

I stress the importance of being accurate because within most STEM disciplines there are ethical boundaries that can easily be crossed by giving out false information. Early on in my engineering career, the questions I was being asked while on a project site frequently dealt with safety. When handling a project in the health care industry, for instance, the code is very detailed. A lot of engineering firms do not handle health care work precisely because of how detailed the procedures are when dealing with human life. For example, electrical engineering firms must account for the hospital emergency power infrastructure system. In order to maintain the integrity of the emergency generator system, only certain pieces of equipment are permitted to be connected to it. If a piece of equipment is incorrectly connected to the generator system, it could literally mean the difference between life and death for a hospital's patients. The liability is huge. To this day, if I have any doubt about whether my answer is 100 percent accurate, I never hesitate to let the client know I will get back to them after I've checked and double-checked my answer. I'm willing to risk looking like an engineer who is unsure of herself in the short term for the long-term benefits of proving to clients and coworkers alike that my final answers are words they can trust.

⊘ Be reasonable

As I mentioned earlier in this chapter, people—male and female—make mistakes. If someone assumes we hold a job title other than the one we do, it probably was an honest mistake. Have you ever asked someone in a store for help only to find out that person didn't work there? Why did you ask them for help? Because of the way they were dressed? Because they "looked the part"? Mistakes happen. When it happens to us as females in a STEM workplace, we should simply inform the person that we are not who they believe us to be and ask if we can help by directing them to the right person. The majority of the time, their assumptions are not spiteful; there is no reason for a simple misunderstanding to damage our self-confidence or evoke a negative response.

One such story comes from Cecilia, an acquaintance who now works for a well-respected civil engineering firm in Carson City, Nevada. Cecilia, who has more degrees than I can count—including the second advanced geodesy degree ever earned by a woman from her native country—is an incredibly experienced and talented civil engineer. When she was a visiting scientist for six months at a jet propulsion lab in Pasadena, California, there were multiple times when she would be standing by a copy machine, a man would burst into the room and bark orders about how many copies he needed, and ask when she could get to it. Not only did this happen more than once, but it was the same man each time! Even though Cecelia politely explained each time that making copies was not part of her job description as a visiting scientist, she eventually felt compelled to avoid standing near photocopiers to resolve the situation.

⊘ Be realistic

Just because a man chooses to pursue a STEM career does not make him radically different from other men, just as our choosing to follow STEM careers does not make us radically different from the general female population. Therefore, most of the general attitudes and attributes displayed by men outside of STEM disciplines are mostly true of men within STEM disciplines, and we must come to accept that.

In my experience, men do not give as many compliments as women do; it's just not a dominant gene of theirs. Because of this we often feel unsupported in the workplace because our male coworkers rarely share their gratitude or their encouragement. We may not hear a lot of "atta girls." Therefore, we should be prepared for the likelihood that if a limited number of female coworkers are around, there could also be a limited number of encouraging words and actions.

In school, the high grades we earned reassured us that we were doing good work. As employees in a male-dominated workforce, not getting yelled at can sometimes be about the closest thing to encouragement we might find. Not all generalizations are always true, of course. We can get lucky and work in a firm where men feel comfortable giving compliments when they are due.

Hearing that we are doing a good job can boost our confidence, but it does not mean we are doing poorly if we don't often receive accolades. For me, the compliments and encouragements at TJ Krob were few and far between, which, sadly, fed into my self-doubt and damaged my confidence. True, without the reaffirmation of our peers, doubt can build inside of us. But we can learn to embrace the doubt and use it as motivation to make sure we take our jobs seriously and perform at our best.

Initially when I went to work for Tom, my confidence was damaged just by the numerous comments he made about the set of plans I had prepared. I thought that I had dotted all my i's and crossed all my t's. At first I took his critiques as a blow to my ability as an engineer. Over time, however, my plans got better and Tom had less and less constructive criticism. For myself, I over-prepared for every project to ensure that I was equipped to do the best job possible. Tom's way of communicating that I was doing a good job was to increase my salary (which is always welcome) and to write what I consider high markings on my yearly review. When I am doing a plan review for one of my employees, I make sure to provide verbal positive affirmation as well. Always look for the positive and recognize and reward people accordingly.

Finding our confidence and maintaining it on the job is difficult, especially early in our careers. Chapter six explores the obstacles that can crush our confidence and highlights strategies to overcome them.

CONCLUSION

When working with men, earning their respect takes hard work and, more important, patience. Just as all new employees have to prove to their coworkers that they belong and are capable, females in STEM fields have to prove they've earned their professional place among the men. Communication patterns in some environments, such as meetings, have been established to meet the needs of men, and we—being the minority—usually have to adapt. Even as we advance in our jobs, which I will discuss in the next chapter, we will likely continue to find pushback from our male coworkers, clients, or visitors. Whether that pushback is intended or not is unimportant. What is important is not allowing it to damage our self-confidence.

For inspiration, tools, and resources, visit www.UnlockingYourBrilliance.com and www.STEMspire.org.

Chapter 5

MOVE ON UP—AND LOVE IT

I was working far more than forty hours a week for Tom Krob and taking on more and more responsibility. The real-world applicable knowledge I was gaining under his tutelage was incredible. After about two years, I was promoted through the ranks at TJ Krob to become a project manager. The overall success of projects now depended on my abilities both as an engineer *and* as a leader of the small team I directed. If there was a hole in any part of the process, I had to face the questions from above and quickly come up with solutions.

I remember welcoming the new level of responsibility and accountability when I was promoted. And I assumed the new title of *project manager* would change how male coworkers and clients perceived me. In fact, it did little to change or boost my credibility.

Whether consciously or subconsciously, my male coworkers were showing signs that they did not believe I was capable of handling the responsibility that came with my career advancement. This persistent bias can be damaging to the self-confidence of women in STEM fields, which is something we desperately need in order to tackle the growing responsibility as we advance in our careers.

In our fields, we have little choice but to find ways to work and feel comfortable among men. The strategies presented in this chapter touch on behaviors that can help when we progress to positions that require us to supervise male employees.

THE HURDLE: FINDING THE GUTS AND GUSTO TO RISE THROUGH THE RANKS

I think it is safe to say that we all want to advance in our careers. Females in STEM careers are typically a motivated bunch. After all, it takes a specific desire to voluntarily enter industries that men typically dominate. The desire to prove that we are capable is powerful and keeps us motivated to advance. Whether we are trying to make more money, earn a more respectable title, gain a new leadership position, or become a business owner, our major career advancements inevitably come packaged with uncertainty. Within this uncertainty, however, we often find the biggest career opportunities.

At some point along our career paths, we are likely to find ourselves faced with a promotion opportunity that would require us to manage male employees as opposed to simply working among them. If we impress our bosses enough to be promoted into a management position, we are qualified to monitor the work of all employees, female and male. But staff acceptance of this reality won't come easy. Male managers will likely make it known that they disapprove of females performing the same duties; so, too, will the males we are leading.

At the time that I was promoted to project manager, I was the only female engineer in the office. My responsibilities included managing the projects the other engineers and designers were working on. I was excited to be in this position and thrilled that Tom Krob thought I had progressed enough that I was now ready for this added responsibility. My male colleagues, on the other hand, weren't exactly thrilled with the idea that I got promoted and they didn't. They weren't rude or disrespectful; they just didn't show any additional respect for me in my new role. I tried not to let it bother me, demonstrated a confident and positive attitude, and just continued with my job.

By this time in my life, I had married my high school sweetheart and we had a child on the way. My relationship with my husband was not great, and that was taking a toll on me personally. Not only did I face a lack of respect from my male coworkers, I also faced a lack of respect from my husband. One time he belittled me by shouting that my engineering degree and job position meant nothing. Stay tuned.

STRATEGIES FOR MAKING IT THROUGH

Advancing in our careers gives us a sense of accomplishment and success, which is important for maintaining our drive and interest in our work. Most of us do not join the workforce and feel content with the first position we take. We have hopes of being promoted into positions with more responsibility and more rewards. Rarely do those promotions come at just the right time or exactly when we are ready for them.

In STEM fields, advancement opportunities can come quickly, in large part because the skills and abilities are valuable and highly transferable across a variety of jobs (Georgetown University Center on Education and the Workforce, 2011). But we may not feel entirely prepared for advancement right as the opportunity presents itself. So what's a girl to do? The following strategies can help ease the doubt we may experience at just such a moment in our careers.

⊘ Confront the uncertainty

Sometimes the amount of confidence that has taken us to where we are may not be enough to get us to where we want to be. It takes time and effort to convince ourselves that we can take that next big step in our careers.

After serving as a project manager in the Las Vegas office for four years, the next major transition in my career came when TJ Krob landed a major job in northern Nevada working with the Lyon County School District. Hired by an architect who worked with Lyon County, we were asked to integrate lighting and electrical systems into a number of new and expanding schools. Although this was just one client, the contract amounted to several major jobs. Those major jobs demanded constant oversight and soon required us to consider opening an office in Reno, much nearer to where the construction was taking place. Tom and I had an open, in-depth discussion over the course of several months about the possibility of opening the office in Reno. It made sense that if we were to open a Reno office, I was the logical one to move there and run the office. Tom left the decision up to me; he would support whatever I decided to do. I was hesitant because I would be starting over in a new town where I knew only a few people. I would have to go through a couple of years of trying to prove myself again. Did I have the energy to do this?

After traveling between Reno and Las Vegas a number of times, I decided I would move north under one condition: I would become owner of the new operation in Reno. I did not want to make such a big change in my life and continue working for someone else. I was the person who was working on the northern Nevada projects and was most familiar with the clients. I knew this would be an incredible opportunity for me. However, I didn't want to go if I wasn't going to have a part of the company and a say in how things were done. Tom was very supportive of this idea. We agreed that we would form a separate company. This was the beginning of PK Electrical, Inc.

Tom was going to remain in Las Vegas, and I was going to be responsible for all of our projects in northern Nevada. Because of everything I had learned from Tom, I had developed the itch to start my own private engineering firm. The only problem that arose was, well, I didn't know anything about starting a business!

Before the opportunity in Reno arose, I had never seriously thought that I could become my own boss and run my own business. As an employee at TJ Krob, I had watched my boss and mentor for years, but that did not mean I could mimic his abilities. After all, I watched him *run* a business; I was never able to watch him *start* a business. The world of S corporations, tax ID numbers, buy-sell agreements, and such was completely new to me, and I had a long list of questions to prove it. Not being well versed in business was enough to have me second-guessing my abilities to run my own firm, but something inside of me drove me to pursue the opportunity. I spoke with my entrepreneurial father at length numerous times regarding the move to Reno. He provided the positive affirmation I was looking for: he thought it was a great opportunity for me to thrive, and he was confident I would be successful. After all, entrepreneurialism is in my blood.

I was nowhere near being adequately prepared to take the giant step into business ownership, and I knew I was bringing on a flurry of additional work and responsibility. But once I presented the idea to Tom, I backed it up with a bundle of research that showed him I was serious. Then, in January 1996, with me as 51 percent co-owner and Tom as 49 percent co-owner, we established PK Electrical, Inc. I was preparing to head up a new business in a new city with new people to whom I needed to prove my capabilities. After spending six years in Las Vegas, I had become comfortable with all of the contractors and the businesses we had as clients. Now, in Reno, I was essentially starting over. Other than watching Tom for six years and growing up with my dad as an entrepreneur, I had no clue how to run a business. I asked a lot of questions, read a lot of books, and simply applied practical knowledge.

Even with all of my prior study and planning, I was not mentally prepared for the amount of work required to start a business. The documentation alone can be a real headache. There were attorneys and accountants who helped the process go more smoothly, but I had to put in the sweat equity in order to get the PK Electrical ball rolling. I thought I had done enough research to keep me well informed. Nope. As I was asked to answer endless questions, I wished I had done more so that I could have limited the uncertainty and known exactly how I wanted to form the new company.

Going from *employee* to *boss* is a difficult transition. Thankfully, I had the advantage of being a project manager under Tom before I managed PK Electrical in its entirety in Reno. The managerial

experience prepared me somewhat, but once I had the responsibility of being a business owner, I experienced the pressure of knowing my actions could make or break the company. Every day was a new day and a learning opportunity. I applied what I had learned the day before to the current day, hoping it would make me a better, smarter business owner.

Ruth Charney, president-elect of the Association for Women in Mathematics and professor at Brandeis University, refers to what I was going through as imposter syndrome. "Everyone, including those big shots in your field who seem to know everything, has had a crisis of confidence. As graduate students, we all wondered if we could really do this stuff—and if so, would we be any good at it? Even after we got jobs, we were convinced that we were not really as good as people thought we were. And the better the job, the more convinced we were that we didn't belong there. The imposter syndrome is rampant!"

Ruth reminds young women in STEM careers that if they have doubts about themselves, to "remember that you are in good company . . . *very* good company. With luck, the feeling will subside as you get older, but it never goes away. Don't be afraid to share your concerns with your friends and mentors. They probably have some good stories to tell about themselves. I recently served on a panel in which well-established, successful scientists discussed their own experiences with the imposter syndrome. It was a real eye-opener for the audience of young and aspiring scientists."

Tracy Drain is familiar with the syndrome. When she began at Jet Propulsion Laboratories, she was a junior engineer working on a team of much more experienced engineers. "I knew very little about spacecraft design, verification, and operations when I started," Tracy said. "I'd studied mechanical engineering in school, and everything I learned about what needs to be done to get a mission off the ground I learned on the job at JPL." After several years of working on her first flight project, "I'd learned a huge amount about various aspects of the life cycles of a project," Tracy said, "and a great deal about things specifically related to that project."

Eventually, the lead systems engineer joined another project. Tracy said she was hesitant about applying for the job, because "while I'd learned a lot about the mission and felt technically experienced enough, I was nervous about the idea of taking on such a leadership role," she says.

So she consulted with her managers "to ensure I understood everything that would be expected from me," Tracy remembered. "Then I sought the advice of several more senior engineers that I had worked with, to talk through the pros and cons. The most useful piece of advice I received was that it is *usually* not a good idea to take on a new job that has more than fifty percent technical/ management tasks that are new to you. If it is more than that, you should learn who else would be on the team, and whether they have strengths in areas that are new to you—so that as a complete team, the learning curve isn't too steep."

Tracy also spoke to the people who would be her immediate superiors. "I asked them why they considered me to be a good candidate when there were other engineers with more technical experience and expertise than I had," Tracy said. "I learned that they'd noticed I'd developed a great working relationship with the people on the systems engineering team, as well as the people on other teams across the project. So even though I wasn't the person with the deepest technical experience, they saw my ability to interact well with the other engineers and scientists as a key asset for this particular job."

Tracy accepted the promotion, and never regretted her decision. "I found that I was better at it than I thought I would be," she
said, "and I lived up to the expectations of my managers. I've often
been told that I underestimate my own abilities. As they say, we
are our own worst critics. But I would advise everyone not to shy
away from seeing themselves in a leadership position, just because
they think they aren't yet ready for a certain level of responsibility."

⊘ Build a supportive work team

As women involved in the STEM fields, we share the common goal
of increasing the female presence across the different industries
that remain male-dominated. If we rise through the ranks to reach
a position with hiring responsibilities, we will face an interesting
dilemma: Do we hire females simply to help level the imbalance?

As we do our part to attract and retain females in STEM fields,
we have to be careful not to "overcorrect" and adopt gender biases
that go in the opposite direction. Nowhere else is this more evident
than in the hiring process. We want to give females the chance to
become successful in STEM careers, but we would be doing our
companies a disservice if we didn't hire the most qualified appli-
cant regardless of gender. By hiring the best candidate for each
position, we ensure progress in the areas of science, technology,
engineering, and math.

Nancy Knowlton, Sant Chair for Marine Science at the
Smithsonian Institute and former board member of the American
Association for the Advancement of Science, noted, "These days,
I think gender imbalance is less of a problem than it used to be, as
women hold more and more positions of leadership. But, I do feel

that women tend to be more cooperative and men more competitive. As a result, when someone asks, 'Who is the best person for such-and-such?' often a man comes to mind first. This is something that is not going to go away any time soon—it may be in our DNA. So the best strategy is to remember to not just go with the person who is most conspicuous."

Back in 1997, projects were slowly but surely starting to come through the doors of PK Electrical. Having the projects with Lyon County School District helped my company establish credibility and attract new customers. I was able to use them as a reference, and once some of our projects were constructed, potential clients could see our work and our commitment to northern Nevada. The extra work enabled me to hire my first employee, Alan Wiskus. I needed an employee with a specific skill set from within the industry. Alan was one of two men who applied. With his wide background in medical, educational, industrial, and commercial projects, Alan came on as a very capable electrical designer. Little did I know it at the time, but Alan would become an ideal business partner and unconditional supporter of both my company and me.

Hiring Alan helped smooth out the obstacles that are common in starting a new business; he complemented my strengths from the very beginning. We have similar philosophies about running a business and our personalities work well together. Because Alan and I were aware that we needed to control the company's growth, we were able to responsibly move PK Electrical in the right direction. Without controlled growth, the rapid progression could have been overwhelming and our new vulnerable company might have collapsed.

Hiring talented, responsible employees is only one part of the puzzle when building a supportive team. In chapter six, I will address other strategies for strengthening support outside of the office.

I believe very strongly in fostering a team environment and in building my employees' confidence and capabilities. Each year during the first week of January, we have a team alignment day. The purpose of this day is to get us out of the office, away from the phones and the e-mail, and to get our entire team aligned with our company goals. It also allows everyone to set and focus on personal goals for the year. It is an open forum in which all staff members express themselves freely.

We also offer a professional development program for which we give each staff member a yearly budget that may be spent on improving his or her professional and personal skills. Staff can attend these classes and seminars during work hours.

⊘ Client relationships are key

While this strategy can be applied across all major industries (as client relationships directly impact your business), building relationships with clients is different for a woman in a male-dominated field.

When I started PK Electrical, here came a native Pennsylvanian opening a business in the wilder west. In fact, Reno was just about as far as I could travel from where I grew up and still be in the same country. With Alan also a nonnative of Nevada, we had no choice but to grow our client relationships from the first impressions we made forward.

It's challenging to earn the trust of new clients in a new market, especially if they are all of the opposite sex and have never worked with a woman in your position. The atmosphere in Reno in the late 1990s was still primarily what I'd refer to as a club of good ol' boys. Business executives all seemed to know one another and only refer business among their chummy confederation. I was the new girl on the block and had to prove the capability of my firm to the town's already established architects, contractors, construction firms, and engineers—nearly all of whom were men. It took a great deal of patience to network in the new market. Thankfully, Alan was more than willing to hit the golf courses in the name of PK Electrical, using that time-honored "business lubricant" to introduce the establishment to our new firm.

From the very beginning, Alan and I knew that strong customer service could set our firm apart from our competition. To this day, we ensure that we are not just talking about customer service but acting on it because it is what we believe in. If a client ever has a complaint about any part of our work, we do not waste our time arguing about how it was not our fault. Rather, we own up to whatever it might be and aim to get it fixed quickly and professionally.

It is not a complicated equation that has happy clients coming back for repeat business or referring others to your business. But top-notch customer service is something that is often neglected by new business owners. Once a client gives your business a chance, you have the opportunity to prove yourself and exceed their expectations. In a new market you will likely only get that one chance to keep a client, however. If your work product is consistently top quality and trustworthy, your new clients will help you establish and grow your business by funneling other business your way, which is why client relationships are so vital.

⊘ Adopt a management style that suits you

Because I was never comfortable around bosses who overtly tried to intimidate me, I have adopted a management style that

encourages dialogue and shows consideration for those I supervise. Even so, I have had my share of frustrations with employees
who behaved differently toward me than they would with a male
superior. For instance, a key designer of mine once resigned from
PK Electrical via e-mail! In his message he briefly explained that
he was going to pursue other career opportunities outside of engineering, which was fine. What was not acceptable was the fashion
in which he quit: no notice, no face-to-face discussion, and he slid
his key through the front door slot when I was out of the office. I
was particularly frustrated with him because I have an open-door
policy with all of my employees. To add to my frustration, the
designer told a major client of ours to contact another manager
in my office (a male) about finding a replacement designer for the
project he'd been working on. This employee had plenty of chutz-
pah when it came to undermining my authority even though he
was too timid to talk to me in person when he resigned.

Fortunately, it ended well. I spoke with the other manager and
we immediately contacted the client and set up a conference call to
discuss the situation. I reassured the client that our company had
the capable staff necessary to meet their deadline while providing
a high-quality project. I made sure that I sounded confident. By
the end of the call they were satisfied and the project continued
without incident.

There is no way to learn the pitfalls of the countless management styles without experience. I do all I can to ensure that my
employees know what I expect from them. If something does not
get done, it affects the entire company. Alan and I try to foster a
team-oriented environment that has us all relying on one another.
We find that we do not have to micromanage, something we both
despise anyway. We try to hire capable people and allow them to
do what they were hired to do, but this takes a lot of accumulated

trust. I respect my employees and believe that they can do their jobs without me watching over their shoulders and critiquing them. Of course, this style comes with its dangers. If we hire an employee because we think he or she can operate without being heavily monitored and that does not prove to be true, we have to find a solution or face losing major production. I cannot change the environment in which PK Electrical operates simply because one employee is not performing.

Over the years, we have developed a list of interview questions to help us find appropriate team members. If an engineer is applying for an open position, we also ask this person to take a short test that has practical problems we face every day. We contact references and look at a portfolio of the candidate's previous projects if available. However, our process isn't perfect. Every once in a while one gets past us and we later learn that the person does not possess the skills needed for the specific job. We have a ninety-day probationary period, with a review at the completion of the ninety days. That's our opportunity to address any issues in an open forum. We also do yearly reviews in the same manner. We try to provide as much assistance as possible to improve skills. However, if it's not working, we unfortunately have to terminate the employee.

☑The title is not enough

When I became a business owner, instead of hoping that a great weight would be lifted and my challenges would be over, I approached my new role as inviting greater responsibility and more challenges into my work life. That way, when the obstacles multiplied, I was better prepared to handle them. Following that same philosophy, I have never used my title as business owner as an excuse to sidestep a challenge or avoid explaining myself for any reason. Never get caught using "Because I'm the owner, that's why" as an acceptable answer to any question.

Even when I started PK Electrical as 51 percent owner, I still saw myself as an employee of Tom Krob, who then owned 49 percent. It can be a difficult transition going from the employer-employee relationship to becoming partners. Over time it became easier to accept. In 2005 I purchased another 9 percent of the company stock and Alan purchased the remaining stock from Tom. I still have a great relationship with Tom today. He will always be a mentor to me, and I do feel his respect for me has grown. He has observed what we have done with PK Electrical, how well admired PK is in the community, and has witnessed the top-notch quality of work and customer service we provide. To this day, if I have a question, whether business or engineering related, I don't hesitate to reach out to Tom. I am forever grateful that this man came into my life.

My feeling of still being Tom's employee may have been due to my low self-confidence and self-esteem at the time, which I now attribute to the abusive personal relationship I was in, the new responsibilities of being a business owner, and the feeling of practically starting over in a new city. Initially I moved by myself to Reno with our daughter, Alyssa. My husband wasn't moving up to Reno for another six months. Here I was, a single mom of sorts, without any support. Those six months allowed me to give a lot of thought to the type of relationship I was in and whether I wanted to continue dealing with the verbal abuse that I had become accustomed to. I decided that I needed to seek out a professional counselor with whom I could discuss these issues.

Talking with professionals has allowed me to build my confidence and clarify what I want out of life. I want to be happy. I want my daughter to be happy and I don't want her to witness or grow up in a household with inappropriate behaviors. My husband did move to Reno after the six months. Within one year of that, we were separated and had filed for divorce. Believe it or not, this bolstered my confidence.

Continuing with my personal journey, I met my current husband, Jeff, in Reno while working together. He is an architect. He is also the most amazing, caring, and supportive man. We were married in 1999, and a year later our daughter, Sydney, was born. Jeff tells me constantly how proud he is of me and provides the emotional support that I need. This helps me every day to express and show my confidence. I will provide more detail about my family and their support in chapter seven.

As you move forward in your career, there is a fine line between having the confidence to embrace a new position and letting the position go to your head. Also, having a prestigious title does not mean its holder always has the answers. I have never lost my ability to ask questions. It is easy to assume that people think someone in my position should have all the answers, but I do not always have the *right* answers. I still value finding the accurate information as much as I did my first day on the job as an electrical engineer. Asking questions does not strip away any of my credibility.

CONCLUSION

Rising through the ranks can be very exciting, exhilarating, and terrifying. For me, it was one of the most exceptional career opportunities. When I first started managing others, I found that I was good at it and was able to build on my success by opening the office in Reno. But I didn't do it alone; I credit Tom Krob for mentoring me along the way and providing the foundation that I needed. One of the best decisions I made was to hire Alan back in 1997. Surrounding yourself with the right people who help you flourish as a person, manager, or owner is important. Alan and I share very similar business philosophies. With the support of people like Tom and Alan, combined with my own empowerment of self, I have been STEMspired to achieve that meteoric rise.

No matter which stage they might be at in their careers, females in male-dominated fields will often report that it is difficult to maintain their confidence. There have been countless times I have temporarily lost my confidence along my career path. It can be easy to let our confidence slip when we are attempting to stand out in a field that was built by—and is still run by—the opposite sex. Without confidence, we can find ourselves contemplating leaving our jobs or, more drastically, leaving the STEM fields all together. For this reason, I have dedicated the following chapter to the importance of maintaining our confidence.

For inspiration, tools, and resources, visit www.UnlockingYourBrilliance.com and www.STEMspire.org.

Chapter 6

HOLD YOUR HEAD HIGH

T hroughout my six years in Las Vegas, I often doubted whether or not I had enough knowledge to complete the jobs Tom was assigning me. This had a lot to do with me second-guessing, and sometimes even doubting, my abilities. Over the first few months in Reno, I experienced a different kind of doubt: whether or not I had the energy and confidence to oversee every facet of a new business. I worked long hours and constantly feared that I might be overlooking something. While the Lyon County School District projects were under way in a number of smaller towns, the thought that the life of PK Electrical primarily relied on one client had me double- and triple-checking every aspect of every project. As a new business owner, my confidence in my knowledge and abilities was crucial. I had to find ways to maintain and build my confidence in order for others to believe in my business.

THE HURDLE: MAINTAINING CONFIDENCE IN GOOD TIMES AND BAD

While some level of confidence is in our genes, working on actively building and maintaining it is imperative to thriving in the workforce, especially one dominated by men. We may find that the confidence we developed during our undergraduate and graduate studies is easily squashed when we are thrown into a hostile work environment.

Maintaining your confidence at all levels throughout your career is important, especially as a leader. In my opinion, showing a lack of confidence helps others buy into the notion that women do not belong in the STEM fields. When I was a project manager, there were times I just wanted to go into the bathroom and cry, but I didn't. Instead, I took a deep breath and refused to let others intimidate me. As women we need to let our work do the talking. Showing someone that we are capable and confident in our work speaks much louder than words. By constantly performing our jobs at a high level, we will prove our abilities and help build our confidence.

I am a strong proponent of peer groups because through them you can build your confidence in a less intimidating crowd. The Society of Women Engineers (SWE) is a great example. Founded sixty years ago, SWE (pronounced *Sweeeee!*) is an organization that encourages women to succeed in engineering. This is a peer group of all women, all with an interest or career in engineering. Attend the local section meetings, speak to other members, or volunteer on a committee. The relationships that are built at these peer groups will help provide the support that is needed.

For me, my biggest confidence builder has been the Entrepreneurs' Organization (EO). Talk about an intimidating situation and a confidence builder all at the same time; how about having other business owners, all male, know the ins and outs of not only your business but also your personal life? Presenting issues to them that come up at work or at home and being held accountable by them has truly helped me become a more confident and successful business owner, manager, and person. The relationship that I have with this group of peers means the world to me. I know that if I am ever in doubt, they can help me confront the issue and move forward in a positive and confident manner.

As I discussed in chapter three, mentorship is an important approach for building and maintaining your confidence. Just as with the peer groups, a one-on-one mentor can bring huge benefits. The majority of successful women time and time again credit their participation in some sort of mentorship program for dramatically helping them reach their career goals.

For me, Tom Krob was as intimidating a boss as a woman could have. He was fair, but stern. He pushed me as hard as I would go, and I was frightened of disappointing him. It took time to gain his trust, yet there was no way for his employees to earn his trust besides proving themselves through hard work. Outside of asking a lot of questions, I kept to myself and worked as hard as I could. I was the only female engineer Tom ever hired, and I felt like I had to show him that he made the right decision by hiring me.

During our first few years in the workforce, identifying confidence builders can be difficult. This chapter is dedicated to pointing out a number of strategies for maintaining our confidence throughout challenging times during our careers.

STRATEGIES FOR MAKING IT THROUGH

As women, we have to be confident in our abilities before anyone else will be. If we are not, we will be unable to prove to others that we are capable of the role we have been hired to fill. Our confidence is our lifeblood. Without it, we begin to second-guess that we have made the right decisions within our careers, which, in turn, inhibits us from making clear choices moving forward.

We recognize that vocalized praise and encouragement may not be readily available as we progress through our careers in predominantly male STEM fields. So what's a girl to do? The following are some tips that focus on areas—networking groups, extracurricular activities, and our families—in which we can find support and use it to build the confidence we need to realize our full potential in our chosen disciplines.

⊘ Join a support group

Like most people, I am more confident when I surround myself with people who believe in me. When I joined the EO in 2006, I was exposed to an extraordinary group of talented business owners. I was searching for a supportive group and was pleased to find that at every chapter level—local, regional, or national— the positive environment was contagious. Although the group is not engineering specific, I cannot put a price on the tips and best practices I have learned through my involvement and have incorporated into my own line of work.

Each and every EO member is open to helping me resolve any challenges I may be experiencing. The support from EO members has helped me overcome major hurdles in my personal life as well as some of the most difficult situations I have encountered in the working world. For example, I dread everything that terminating an employee entails. I used to silently hope the pressing issues behind the need for firing someone would go away on their own, but they never do. In one specific instance, I had an employee who was unproductive and costing PK money. He was competent; he just was not a good fit for how PK operated. Alan and I fretted over dismissing this employee for about six months because we both dislike the responsibility of firing staff that comes with our positions. I finally brought the issue up in confidence to fellow EOers. We talked openly about it and treated it like any other problem that needed solving. The members offered me their best practices concerning termination, and I've been able to confidently apply them to any situation ever since.

Looking back at the anxiety that built up because of my indecision, I now know that putting it off was the worst thing to do in that situation. When Alan and I finally fired this employee, he begged to stay at first but finally went peacefully. Six months of stress were all wrapped up in a rather brief and uneventful finale.

Because tempers can be hot in termination situations, I never fire anyone alone. Though I adopted this practice very early on, I was very pleased I had Alan with me during one particular employee termination years into PK's existence. Alan and I met with the employee we were terminating and the actual event turned out to last only about a minute. The woman walked in, sat down, and as we began talking she immediately got the message, stood up, and stormed out the door. It was the events surrounding the actual termination, however that had me thankful Alan always helped with the firings. Before her termination, the woman had made it known around the office that she had a concealed weapons permit and often carried a gun with her. While she may not have been malicious (thank goodness) and her gun never made an appearance, she was somewhat unscrupulous. After her termination, she sent me a pretty nasty and threatening e-mail because we disputed her unemployment claim. In a poor attempt to give her accusatory e-mail credibility, she had carbon copied an e-mail address that suggested a lawyer from a well-known law office was also receiving the e-mail. I right-clicked on the address, however, and it revealed the real recipient's identity: her brother-in-law, who was not a lawyer.

All in all, the assistance that can be found within an enduring peer group is irreplaceable. EO works for me, but it took effort on my part to find a group that was the right fit. Surrounding yourself with like-minded individuals who have similar goals can help build your confidence exponentially. In contributing valuable advice to respected peers in the forum setting, you become increasingly confident about presenting yourself as credible to your partners, clients, and superiors.

If you decide a professional support group is right for you, talk to your peers. Ask them what groups they are involved with and whether or not it might be right for you. Do your research to determine which groups are available in your area and visit a handful. When searching for the right peer group, the following tips can help you select a group that matches your overall goals. I identified the groups that I wanted to be a part of by attending one of their meetings. I was able to meet a few people and ask questions. I also looked online and read about each group.

THE LEADERSHIP

Though you may be committed to putting in personal time and effort for your group, your dedication will be irrelevant if you are not taking away any value. Therefore, it is important to analyze how the group is led. By looking at the structure of the group, you should be able to assess the commitment of the group's leaders. If their commitment does not match or surpass your own, you will need to look elsewhere. Make sure there is organization all the way through the group, especially at the leadership level. Ensure that steps have been taken to develop a positive, encouraging environment. Getting the most out of the time you spend with your group will require solid leadership on their part.

THE FEES

When taking into account the various membership dues of different business groups, view them as an investment toward advancing your career. While you cannot judge a group solely on the fees it charges, you should be able to assess what the fees cover for each group. These groups should be transparent and make it easy for you to understand how your membership dues are spent. Typical expenses for a group can include meeting space rental, name badges, outings, and recruitment efforts. In addition, many groups donate end-of-year balances to a nonprofit that has values similar to the organization's.

Just as your fees can be considered an investment, so, too, can your time spent with the group. View your commitment as time invested in strengthening the relationships that will help tremendously with finding success in your career.

THE PEOPLE

Lastly, when selecting a support group, be sure to consider whether or not the group is made up of people you could potentially enjoy being around. You are going to be investing your time within this network of professionals; struggling to tolerate the people in your support group will be counterproductive to your goals. By joining a group in which you find you have a difficult time trusting the other members, you will be limiting the value of your membership in the organization because you may not feel comfortable sharing information. From the initial meeting with a new group, you should feel that the members are approachable and trustworthy.

⊘ Own your expertise

Throughout my career, particularly as I emerged from under the umbrella of Tom's tutelage and began to run my own company, I became more comfortable taking on leadership roles and offering my expert opinion. It was a critical transition, and one that helped build my confidence immensely.

Susan Fitzpatrick, president of the Association of Women in Science, believes that resilience is key to these types of transformations. "Culturally, we're not thought of as being resilient," she stated. "As you go along in your career, the challenges tend to get harder, not easier. You feel that with each hurdle you pass, it will get easier—but it doesn't."

One reason that things can get progressively harder for women, Susan feels, is that male mentors' support changes over time. "Male mentors are often very supportive of you during your protégé status. There's a bit of a paternalistic relationship that exists. But as you start to ascend and transition into becoming a peer, suddenly you're up for the same prizes, positions, and promotions that your mentor is seeking. Now you've become a rival, and they have to see you differently. No longer are you someone they're nurturing, protecting, and encouraging to advance. Now you're their peer, standing shoulder-to-shoulder, eye-to-eye. And that's uncomfortable."

Some women avoid this challenge "by willingly staying in the protégé role forever," Susan said. "No matter how senior they are, they manage to make their male mentors feel comfortable with them. They're the good ol' gals—always cheerful, always willing to fetch a cup of coffee. In other words, they don't expect to receive the perks of their position. But I don't think that's healthy."

Susan thinks women have to be willing to test their personal comfort boundaries and build networks with other women. "You have to resolve to act as though you deserve to be at the level to which you've risen," she said. "You need to be ready to confront people who act surprised to see you at that level. And remember that there is safety in numbers: senior women realize that they need a network as much as junior women need a network. Reaching a hand down to help someone up is important, but so is reaching a hand out to someone at your same level—to discuss strategies, issues, and so forth. You need a circle of women peers, an environment where you can ask each other for advice on successfully dealing with difficult colleagues. So as you rise through the ranks, be sure that you don't shed your women peers at the same time."

Often other women will help you learn how to own your expertise.

⊘ Build networks within your industry

Kristin Lauter, principal researcher and head of the Cryptography Group at Microsoft Research, has at various times had a series of papers rejected. Of those times, she said, "I was very discouraged by what I felt was unfair treatment of my work. But I had to realize that there are a lot of factors at play besides quality in terms of acceptance and recognition of my work. The issue is really with the networks that control the power of the respective publications. There's kind of a game to be played; a network that you have to become a part of in order to be accepted."

Most people in society understand that reality, Kristin said, "But in science, we're led to believe—at least as graduate students—that it's a meritocracy, that we're only evaluated on the basis of the quality of our work. So I think that people fail to realize, particularly at the early stages of their careers, that it's very important to be part of a network, to be connected to the appropriate people in your field and to get that respect."

I discussed the importance of support groups above, but joining a group or groups within your specific discipline can also help you build critical networks. Plus, interacting with and learning from peers who have been involved in situations that are similar to your own can offer targeted help, and relating with others in your field of work can be a relief. Discipline-specific groups are filled with people who have likely encountered your problems, yet because you do not directly work with them, you are free to be candid.

I have found two excellent discipline-specific groups to support me as an electrical engineer. As a participant in the Illuminating Engineering Society (IES), I am part of a global network more than eight thousand members strong. The IES is composed of talented individuals who are, in one way or another, involved in lighting by profession. This group of manufacturers, designers, researchers, and lighting engineers hosts a number of beneficial networking events and tradeshows that connect me with others involved in my line of work.

Even more specific than the IES is my involvement in SWE (which I mentioned earlier). I found out about SWE while I was still in college. Through awards, scholarships, and continued education, SWE helps recognize the tremendous contributions of women as both engineers and leaders. Organizations similar to SWE provide validation for women who take on the challenge of working in a career that is dominated by males. Female-specific groups can provide focused support for very specific issues.

☑ Engage in extracurricular activities

Outside of the office, our team collectively participates in community activities such as volunteering at a local food bank. I also encourage my employees to get out there individually and volunteer. My production manager is very heavily involved in Junior League, for example, and since she became involved in that organization I have seen an increase in her confidence level in dealing with her employees. My business development manager sits on the local chapter's board of the Girl Scouts of the USA. Alan is on the local board of the International Association of Electrical Inspectors. Not only do these activities build confidence, but also at the same time, they are one way we can give back to the community.

And outside of business-related peer groups, there are countless other opportunities to find the support we need to strengthen our bodies, minds, and outlooks—all of which have an impact on our self-confidence. I recommend that each of us just find one or more such extracurricular activities that work with our preferences and busy schedules. For going on five years now, I have been running both recreationally and competitively. When I began running, I was already walking about an hour every day, and I adopted a running regime because it allowed me to challenge myself.

Running provides me with time I can have to myself to work through any problems that are pressing, and I discovered that running in the open air allows me to reflect on the complications within my business and how to address them. If we clearly identify our problems, we can tackle them one at a time and see how correcting them fits into the bigger picture. I find it vital to spend my "down time" partaking in activities I enjoy. While it is important to separate work life from my personal time, running allows me to mentally work through the obstacles I am experiencing on both sides.

☑ Don't overlook the power of family

In addition to joining one or more peer groups and engaging in extracurricular activities, there is another important confidence builder not to be overlooked: your family. My two daughters, Alyssa and Sydney, and my husband, Jeff, are all terrific motivators. After a first marriage that was the complete opposite of supportive, I greatly appreciate the support that my family offers. Having a family who believes in you—whether it is made up of your kids, your parents, your grandparents, your spouse, your closest friends, or all of the above—makes your working life much, much easier.

When you have people in your life who take interest in your accomplishments and provide encouragement, it makes all the difference. The people who criticize you for following your passion are counterproductive to your goals. It does not take long for their criticisms to become personal, which will smash your confidence and place unwanted weight on your shoulders. Life throws enough challenges your way without someone close to you belittling you and your accomplishments. Let your supporters know how much their vote of confidence means to you. Fostering a supportive environment within your family makes for a resource that will forever give and give.

CONCLUSION

Maintaining our confidence throughout our careers is crucial to our success. When our confidence falls short, for whatever reason, it has an impact on our focus and productivity. While we may have built up a level of confidence in school, during internships, or throughout the early stages of our careers, it is continually threatened as our careers progress. Finding support even in the middle and late stages of our careers is incredibly important. New responsibility brings about new challenges and we have to be confident that we have the abilities to reach our full potential.

Without confidence, we find ourselves doubting that we can realistically make it in our fields. This can lead to us leaving the fields, which is a pressing concern that plagues women in STEM careers. Just as attracting talented women to STEM fields is a real challenge, so is retaining them.

For inspiration, tools, and resources, visit www.UnlockingYourBrilliance.com and www.STEMspire.org.

Chapter 7

BELIEVE IN HAVING IT ALL

Having a demanding career does not mean women in STEM specialties have to dismiss the idea of having a family. I knew I wanted to be both an electrical engineer *and* a wife and mother. I also knew wanting to be both simultaneously meant I would be piling on more personal responsibility and inviting more complication into my life. Regardless, by the beginning of 1994, I decided I wanted to have a baby (who turned out to be my first daughter, Alyssa).

At that time I was spearheading a number of projects for TJ Krob. The work was challenging, and I was forced to learn new skills at an accelerated rate. Deciding to have my first child brought about questions I would have to provide answers for: *How will Tom react when I tell him I'm pregnant? How much time can I take off for the pregnancy? If I make a mistake on the job, will everyone automatically attribute it to my pregnancy? Who will stay at home when the baby gets sick, my husband or me? How will clients perceive me when I start to show?* As these questions raced through my head, I began to grasp the enormity of my decision.

THE HURDLE: JUGGLING THE RESPONSIBILITY OF FAMILY LIFE *AND* A DEMANDING CAREER

It should go without saying that it is difficult for professional women to make the decision to have a family life *and* a full-time career. After fully committing ourselves to our work, deciding to have a family can feel like throwing a wrench into the machine we have been sweating to get up and running smoothly. The amount of planning, dedication, and organization it takes to establish a career is overwhelming. Throwing the responsibility of having a family on top of that can create madness. It is common to feel that we will turn our careers upside down if we decide to start a family. This feeling usually sets in around the same time that we have reached stability and are finally feeling some level of balance in our working lives. Bringing a spouse and a screaming, diaper-wearing, needy child into the world sounds like the perfect way to disassemble that balance.

The difficulty with making the decision to have a family comes in large part with the long-term, permanent commitment and changes it would bring. Deciding to have children weighs much more heavily on our lives than does a decision to go skiing in Colorado for a week. We cannot return a child if it does not fit into our schedules like we had originally planned. We are committed to making it work. If our careers become compromised or altered because of a newborn, we cannot put child rearing on hold while we rebalance.

Despite the intense pressure our society places on women to marry and procreate, not every woman feels compelled to have children. Just because we have the necessary reproductive organs does not mean every woman must have children. Susan Fitzpatrick, president of the Association for Women in Science and Vice President of the James S. McDonnell Foundation, is not a parent, and she is concerned that there is "an implicit bias that women with children are the ones doing most of the juggling. It ignores the fact that a woman might be dealing with aging parents, or nieces and nephews who require a lot of her time. She might be heavily involved in her community or involved in various activities with her spouse. Some people might have spouses who have disabilities or life-changing illnesses."

Additionally, Susan is affronted by the notion that women aren't advancing in science because of childcare, a point that has been raised in some discussions about the career progression of women in STEM fields. It seems a bias in the opposite direction to believe that "you can get a PhD in physics and yet not be able to solve your childcare problem. It strikes me as odd that someone might think that a person who is smart and creative enough to achieve at very high levels is not also creative enough to solve this one problem. This kind of thinking clouds the real point— whether society values the contributions of women. Women could solve the childcare issue and find their careers still limited by gender stereotypes." Susan also noted that if workplaces were less artificially rigid, the "childcare issue" would not *be* an issue at all.

We all have demands on our time. Susan's elegantly stated solution? "Finding your angle of repose: the place where you feel you are giving yourself to the things that are really important to you. It all involves choice. All through your life, you're going to have other demands on your time, other things that are important to you, crises and commitments. And we just don't know where those are going to come from. It's up to us to figure out how to solve those problems."

For all of us, reading the stories of others who have managed a balance or discussing the idea with women who have lived through it can be extremely helpful.

STRATEGIES FOR MAKING IT THROUGH

Finding that mystical work-life balance is something that every professional woman with a family struggles with. While you may be too young to be considering having a family at this point in your life, the strategies in this chapter can give you a look at what could possibly be in your future. Dedicating ourselves to our careers on their own already demands most of our time. Finding time for a spouse, regardless of how independent he is, will take some juggling. Squeezing in the demands brought about by having children probably seems impossible. And, on top of it all, finding time to maintain our own sanity can get shoved to the bottom of our lists. However, as I've mentioned throughout this book, women in STEM careers are typically very motivated and are likely to crave that lifestyle of "having it all."

So, if having a family life is important to us, or we believe it could be someday, what's a girl to do? The following are some tips I learned—sometimes painfully—throughout my experience of becoming a wife, a mother, and a full-time career woman. You'll see from these strategies that struggling with work-life balance is nothing new.

⊘ Build a relationship with a supportive spouse

This section could be expanded into an entire book if I were to talk about how to attract the right mate. But, as you will soon read, my track record is not perfect and this is not my area of expertise. However, I know that there are other women in a situation that is similar to what mine was. My hope is that by sharing my story, those women can see they are not alone and take the difficult measures to avoid future hardship.

In 1994, when I had Alyssa, I was still married to my first husband. When Alyssa was two, my then husband and I were deciding whether or not to move to Reno so I could open and manage PK Electrical. Instead of discussing the options, he left the decision completely up to me, which fell right in line with how unsupportive he was with my career. His contract with the Air Force was about to expire, and instead of renewing it, he decided he wanted to work with a computer-training business, which also had an outfit in Reno. So, because he had a job opportunity in both cities, he could not have cared less where we lived.

Right around that time, Alyssa got sick and had to be hospitalized. Her father's reaction was that I would automatically be the one to stay with her in the hospital and he would continue to work. It was not at all that I did not want to be with my daughter while she was sick, but I had a career as well. I did not understand why he immediately put the responsibility on me to take time off from my job to stay with our daughter. At the very least, the responsibility could have been shared. However, that was unacceptable in his mind. Since I was the woman, it was my duty to put my job on hold and take care of our child.

Of course, I did, but we could have discussed which job would have been more impacted by a long absence. We could have alternated days. We could have done a lot of different things, but my now ex-husband was not the negotiating type; he was not even the conversation type. While this is just one specific example of many, the point is that an unsupportive spouse can make "having it all" extremely difficult, if not impossible.

While on paper my ex-husband was still part of my life and my daughter's, he was gone long before the divorce was final. Thankfully, I had terrific support from friends. Even my long-distance friends provided encouragement while I juggled my single-mom responsibilities and simultaneously fought a drawn-out divorce and custody battle. In 1998, I hit my two-year mark as owner of PK Electrical. Through enormous challenges and seemingly unbeatable odds (and the wonderful support that therapy can offer), I had a business that was growing, an ex-husband whose comments I was learning to let go of, and a beautiful four-year-old daughter.

In 2000, when I had my second daughter, Sydney, my world had changed quite a bit. I was happily married to my second husband, Jeff. We became friends through work, and soon it was evident to both of us that there was something more than friendship between us. He proved to be terrific with Alyssa, and he was eager to bring a second child into the equation. Because of the incredible support Jeff offered, my family life was finding stability.

Thankfully, throughout my second pregnancy, Jeff offered additional help at home. He has always been willing to sacrifice his career so that he can be at home with the girls more often. As soon as six weeks after Sydney was born, she was going to the babysitter's, and Jeff and I slipped back into our work schedules. However, if one of the girls got sick and required one of us to be at home, Jeff was terrific about being flexible. When Alyssa's school schedule had her coming home directly afterward, Jeff reduced his hours in the office to accommodate that change.

Jeff and I have reversed roles when compared to traditional couples, but it is what we both want. If Jeff wanted to spend more time at work we would have to talk about it and come up with a compromise that worked for both of us. Just as some women have reversed roles because of their desire to follow a full-time career in STEM, there are men out there who have the desire to be heavily involved in the family duties.

Jeff's situation is the complete opposite of mine. Whereas I am surrounded by men on a daily basis, Jeff is surrounded by women. He will pick up the kids from school with other moms, go to Sydney's dance classes with other dance moms, and attend the EO spouse group with wives of other EOers. He is comfortable with it because it allows him to do what he wants to do—spend time with our girls. Not all men can do what Jeff does because they are not surrounded by people who support their choices. Jeff's network of supportive people is just as important to his success as my support group is to mine. As far as I believe women have come in the workforce, I still find it interesting that Jeff is the only male in many of the different activities he is involved in with the kids.

Because of traditional gender roles, women may find it difficult to find a supportive spouse who is willing to handle more of the household obligations. However, research suggests that stay-at-home dads are on the rise. According to the US Census Bureau, the number of fathers who stay at home full-time has doubled since 2000. Plus, those numbers do not include dads who work even one day a week (US Census Bureau, 2010b).

I do not think that a woman who wants to have a serious career should be held back from also having a family. I found in Jeff someone whose goals are highly compatible with mine, but our situation is only one example. There are many different ways to accomplish both and find balance. There are always solutions.

When both parents have serious careers, it is difficult to decide who will adapt their schedule to take care of the house and children. I believe it should not automatically be put on either spouse because of gender. Both parents take on a huge responsibility when they have a child, and it is important to discuss how each will balance work with family responsibilities. If we want to have both a family and a career, we certainly can, as long as we have strong support.

Lori Polasek, marine mammal scientist and professor at the University of Alaska-Fairbanks, points out that while life for a woman in the field of marine biology can be rewarding, it can also be challenging if that woman is a mother. "My work requires that I spend a lot of time in the field," Lori said, "which means adventures to beautiful, remote locations for weeks at a time to study marine animals. That sounds phenomenal, and it is, until you throw in the complication of having a family at home."

Even with a stay-at-home husband, Lori said she felt guilty leaving her children when they were very young. "I struggled with how to make both work and home life successful," she admitted, remembering how she would pump breast milk to ship home while working on a small research vessel. Sharing cramped quarters with 12 other people meant that privacy was nonexistent. "There were a lot of references to a 'dairy' during the trip," Lori wryly recalled, "but what I was doing for my child was more important than a little chiding."

"A job that requires fieldwork while you have a family is challenging," Lori concluded. "A loving partner is important. Focused time and good communication with your children is imperative. But it's possible to be successful with both, and when it is, it is so rewarding."

Because making the decision to have a child is not one that we are forced to make alone, we must open the discussion with our spouses. Having a child is arguably the biggest decision two people make as a couple, so it is crucial to come to an agreement *together*.

⊘ Learn about the experience

Like most professional women, I never gained a lot of experience being responsible for young children because of my career path. Therefore, I had little personal experience to help me decide if I would be a suitable mother. My brother and I often stayed home together when we were younger. However, being only two years older than him, I would classify our time alone more along the lines of "two kids hanging out" than I would "babysitting." In high school, I did a fair amount of babysitting, but in college I was so consumed with my engineering program and extracurricular activities that I never had the time. Then, after I graduated, I began working and was not often responsible for caring for the young children of friends or family. This meant that when I was considering having my first child, I had no basis for gauging my readiness as a nurturer. Nevertheless, I made up my mind that having children was important to me and that I would find a way to balance it all.

In my career, I had always been so focused on being prepared for any obstacles that might arise. Taking on an extraordinary challenge with which I had little prior experience was hard to comprehend. Deciding to have a child, it takes great faith because of the amount of unknowns. I didn't know how my life would change, how my relationship with my husband would change, how my career would be affected. There is no crystal ball or effective user manual to offer any kind of reliable answers for these unknowns. Instead, you can turn to those who have done it and lived to tell the tale.

When Pamela Brown, dean of the School of Arts and Sciences at the New York City College of Technology, began her career as a chemical engineer in 1979, "it was a male-dominated profession," she remembers. "There were no accommodations for flex hours, part-time work, etc., to achieve career-life balance." When her first daughter was born in 1981, Pamela made the "difficult decision" to quit her job, "taking a break from a career that I loved, in order to stay home full-time with my daughter." Three years later, her family having grown to include a one-year old and a three-year old, Pamela returned to school in order to earn a PhD in chemical engineering, with plans for entering academia.

"I was able to earn a PhD in just under five years," Pamela said, "just after the birth of my son, and returned to working part-time as a chemistry lab instructor when he was in nursery school. A year later, I obtained a full-time non-tenure-track teaching position. Five years later, I changed institutions for a tenure-track position, earned tenure, became the program coordinator of the Chemical Technology Program, and later the Dean of the School of Arts and Sciences."

☑ Be open and honest with your coworkers about your pregnancy

Once we make the decision to have a child, we must be open with those in our workplaces whose job functions may be affected by our pregnancies. I always hate hearing about instances in which women are scared they will lose their jobs if their bosses find out they are pregnant. Such a huge milestone in a woman's life should not mean she has to question her job security. Professional women can still have children. We cannot put off telling those we work for (or work with) that we are pregnant. First of all, our bosses will find out. A pregnancy is not something we can easily hide. Plus, having that amount of stress and fear will wear on us every day, and that is not healthy for our developing babies or us.

Back when I was pregnant with Alyssa, because she was my first child, I was entering into a world that was completely unknown to me. But, like everything else, I had to take it one step at a time. First things first, I had to break the news to my boss.

Tom was hard to read, both as a person and as a boss. I remember being unsure how he would really feel about me missing six weeks, which was the standard time allotted for maternity leave. Even though Tom intimidated me, I knew I needed to get up the nerve to tell him about my pregnancy sooner rather than later. Keeping the secret was weighing on my mind daily. I didn't need to add to the stress by trying to keep my pregnancy a secret from my coworkers. The longer I went without telling Tom, the more I felt as if I was doing something wrong by being pregnant.

For this reason, I recommend being upfront about your pregnancy with those around you. When I finally spilled the news to Tom, it truly ended up being a nonevent. I told him my intention was to have Alyssa, take six weeks off, and then go back to work. He seemed happy for me. Regardless of the personality types of our bosses, supervisors, and coworkers, we can do ourselves a favor and relieve the burden of constantly wondering if others know or will soon find out.

Employers know there is always the possibility that women will take longer than they anticipated or not come back to work at all after their child is born. Employers in male-dominated fields deal with employee pregnancies less often, and it should be expected that they could be more skeptical. It is the woman's responsibility to be open and honest with her employer. If we are straight with them, they will not see it as a risk when we put in for maternity leave. After all, it is a natural part of an employer's job, regardless of how male-dominated the industry may be. If we decide to start a family *and* have a career, then we must own the responsibility. We can aim to show our employers that we will not let one part of our lives drastically impact the other. If we have worked to prove that we are dedicated to our jobs, our employers should not think twice about gladly giving us adequate time off to have our children.

⊘ Prepare for maternity leave

As women in demanding STEM careers, we likely have not experienced six weeks off since we started working in the field. As our scheduled leaves approach, we inevitably start to panic. During my first pregnancy, as my leave got closer I remember thinking that I could not possibly miss six weeks; I was sure my career would turn to dust and blow away. I was overly concerned about my projects and I wanted to be sure that my absence would not slow any of them down.

I remember visiting a job site three weeks before Alyssa was born. There I was, a pregnant woman about to burst, wearing a hardhat and inspecting a large-scale engineering project. I remember thinking, *What the hell am I doing out here?* I felt as if everyone was looking at me, thinking I was lost. At the same time, however, I felt I was nonetheless capable of completing my job without compromising the safety of my child.

I remember constantly trying to gauge how my male coworkers would respond to my six-week absence. Although no one vocalized concern, I was sure that they were displeased I would be out of the office for a month and a half after giving birth. I am positive that young women who aren't employed in male-dominated fields struggle with similar conflicts. However, being one of only a few women at a firm magnifies such issues. None of our male coworkers can relate, and being pregnant puts a spotlight on gender differences. The only thing I could do was diligently prepare for my leave, and that's just what I did up until my doctor put me on bed rest two weeks before Alyssa's birth.

Bed rest was miserable. I missed my work responsibilities and I constantly worried about the progress of my projects. I understood the importance of rest to a successful pregnancy, of course. Once Alyssa was born, it was all worth it. Though I longed for the intellectual stimulation that I was used to at the office and on job sites, I thoroughly enjoyed having the company of my new daughter.

My leave time eventually passed and I was able to get back to work. I stepped back in as a project manager and continued where I had left off. Now, however, my family life was demanding more attention, and I had to learn to find balance between my home life and my career.

☑ Decide whether or not to return to work

Those first six weeks after giving birth are wonderful, if you have planned accordingly. But what about weeks seven and beyond? Getting back to work after having a child is difficult, to say the least. The schedules we have become accustomed to over the previous six weeks have to be dramatically reorganized. Days with a newborn are already long. Finding time to fit in an eight-, ten-, twelve-, or fourteen-hour workday can be near impossible, but it has to be done if being both a career woman and a mother is important to us.

Motherhood affects every woman differently. For professional women, there is a nagging question that gets louder and louder as our maternity leave gets closer to expiring: "How will going back to work impact my new child and my family?" While some women may feel the pressure to put off work and stay with their new child, other women long for adult interaction and cannot get back to work soon enough.

Some of us would be bored to tears if we stayed home with our children all day, every day. On the other end of the spectrum, there are those of us who would be moved to tears just by the thought of leaving our children in order to work. A new child (or a new spouse for that matter) can distract a woman and cause her to direct all of her focus on this person. The decision that we make in college to work in professional careers does not always mesh with our wants and needs years later. Having a child and starting a family can, for some of us, be distracting to the point that we are motivated to leave our careers.

Regardless of the decision we make, the important point is that neither reaction is wrong. We all respond to motherhood in our own individual ways, and it is impossible to predict our choices. Having a child is life altering. Only after we have a child can we be certain of how we will handle the new addition. Becoming a mother changes our priorities, reconfigures our outlooks, and alters the things in our lives we always thought to be certain. Returning to work may be right for one mother and completely wrong for another; we just have to wait and see how we feel once we are faced with the decision. In the event we decide not to return to work, we need to inform our superiors as soon as possible. They put their faith in us while we were pregnant and agreed to grant us the time needed to have our children. If we are uncertain as to whether or not we want to return to our positions, we need to show our respect for our superiors by communicating our indecision and consulting with them.

If we find ourselves ready to return to work as previously planned, we may still be uncertain whether we are making the right choice. Leaving an infant at home while we return to long hours at the office will inevitably be hard, especially when we spent every waking moment of the last six weeks together. Doubting the decision to return to work is natural; we may even feel some level of guilt. But the idea of giving up a career that we worked so hard to attain probably does not make any sense. The drive that makes us successful businesswomen does not just turn off once a child is introduced into the picture. On the other hand, as new mothers, being away from our children for any reason may be difficult to justify. Every moment we are at the office may feel like a moment that is being stolen from our children.

The guilt will subside, especially when our children begin to take part in activities that will occupy their days. Once children are enrolled in preschool, they will have a full day to keep them stimulated and busy, just like their mothers.

⊘ Find time to pursue your passions

In chapter six, I introduced the concept of pursuing extracurricular passions when I mentioned my love for running and how it helps me maintain a work-life balance. In all the juggling we do to please our families and the people we work with and for, it is easy to neglect our own needs. We are the only ones who will suffer if we neglect ourselves, and this makes it easier to cut "us" time. But this has to be part of our scheduling. We have to make time to take care of ourselves or we will be unfit for taking care of others. We must keep ourselves in tune both mentally and physically if we are going to take on such chaotic schedules.

Finding time to do the things we love allows us to relax and enjoy activities that help clear our heads. For me, running is an activity I fit in without fail. Finding activities to spur personal growth is important, even if time is limited. Time is always limited, but by maintaining ourselves we will be better in all aspects of life.

I have found a passion in running half marathons. I have done them all over the United States and even one in Germany. This activity allows our family to travel and it allows me to clear my mind. It keeps me healthy and lets me de-stress.

When I run competitively, I often do so as part of a 200-mile relay team. This is a network of sorts that allows me to work with others to meet specified goals. While winning obviously helps validate the value of the group, simply being an integral part of a team helps boost each member's confidence. Running on a team builds relationships and trust—two things that I have found to be irreplaceable on the business side as well.

⊘ Don't spread yourself too thin

The need to keep a successful family running smoothly runs in our blood. When is the last time you heard a man complaining about having a hard time juggling his career and his marriage, or his career and his family? The responsibility is part of our makeup. When we attempt to have both a successful career and a healthy family, we can spread ourselves thin. It is natural for us to set our expectations for ourselves high—sometimes even out of reach.

We have to be realistic about what we can accomplish. As professionals, we want to give our all to our careers. As mothers, we want to be 100 percent committed to our families. However, we can only juggle so many pins without dropping one. We may have tremendously high expectations for ourselves when it comes to our careers and our families, but at the same time we cannot break down with frustration if we happen to be five minutes late to a meeting or forget to wash a child's favorite pajamas. No matter how much pride we have in ourselves as multitaskers, pins will still occasionally hit the floor.

As children age, their needs and schedules change, which inevitably changes our schedules. The only skill that can combat their ever-changing demands is the ability to be flexible. The most effective mother is the one who is able to successfully find balance.

When we are finding all the time we can to be professionals and family women, we may feel that at times we are taking on too much. We might struggle with the idea that we are not being the best parents we can be because of our jobs. We have to make the decisions that are right for us and we have to make personal choices about what we will and will not miss. For instance, sitting at dance practice for two hours is a waste of time for me.

Trying to do everything without setting boundaries will have us scrambling around and unable to devote 100 percent of our attention to anything. I urge you to find self-acceptance when you miss certain family and work events. Early on this is difficult because we want to do everything, and do everything exceptionally well. It gets easier as time goes on.

During the two decades that Colleen Oresky has worked for one company, she's held many different positions in order "to continue to challenge myself," she said, "but also to balance my desire to be there for my family." Today, Colleen is also on the board of Women in Technology and Women in Aerospace and believes that in order to be successful in one's profession, "you have to be happy at both work and home."

When her children were young, Colleen says she had a "great job, architecting and developing an analytical software system and deploying it in locations around the world. I was able to travel to locations and experience various cultures and meet people that I never would have met otherwise. It was a 24/7 job, but it was very rewarding to see people using your system and having it produce results."

To achieve balance, Colleen included her family in her job whenever possible. "My daughters couldn't understand details," she acknowledges, "but they knew I was developing software that tracked the bad guys. They couldn't go with me when I traveled, but I brought back souvenirs from wherever I went. They learned about the countries, and felt special during show-and-tell at school." Colleen's daughter even advanced in the school Geography Bee when she was able to name the capital of Malaysia, because her mother was in Kuala Lumpur at the time.

For women who wish to balance a family with their career, Colleen advised, "Be passionate about what you do, and share that passion with your family so they understand and feel a part of your work life. Be organized and make changes as necessary, so you're 100 percent at work when you're there, and 100 percent with your family when you're with them. And ask for help: it is not a sign of weakness."

I cannot think of many instances in which I felt completely balanced in terms of work life and family life. There is always something that wants or needs more attention. By establishing boundaries and coming to terms with the things I am content with missing, I have been able to find a balance that works for me. For instance, I do not schedule meetings before 9 a.m. because that is my time to get ready with Alyssa and Sydney.

Having a child and starting a family does not mean we have to hide away our professional aspirations; we may not even have to put them on hold. Having support at home is irreplaceable. This type of life is too much to handle on our own. For those of us who are willing to put in the work, having both healthy family lives and successful work lives is possible—we just have to remember to find time for ourselves somewhere amid the whirlwind.

CONCLUSION

While at times it can be trying, being a mother and having a career are both very important to me. Though initially I may not have known what exactly I was getting myself into, I've learned a lot along the way. For me, the second time around was easier because I knew what to expect with the pregnancy. Having my first daughter answered a lot of the unknowns that you can only truly find out by going through a pregnancy.

Being a mother is extremely rewarding and I am forever thankful that I am able to have a family while also following my career. To ensure that I devote a fair amount of time to both my family and my work, I continue to take organization and planning seriously, which was also important while I was pregnant. I remember managing the elements in which I had some level of control. For instance, I even scheduled my C-section around important meetings!

For women in STEM careers who are thinking of having a child, my best advice is to carefully manage the things we can control. With that said, we also need to have faith that the things we cannot control will manage themselves.

For inspiration, tools, and resources, visit www.UnlockingYourBrilliance.com and www.STEMspire.org.

Chapter 8

LOOKING FORWARD

t is an odd thing for an author to wish for, but deep down I do sincerely hope this book and others like it will be obsolete in ten to twenty years. Why? Because that will mean women have successfully closed the gender gap in male-dominated fields. I hope that even the phrase "male-dominated fields" will no longer exist. While women have made huge strides in expanding their presence in careers overrun by men, we are still far from leveling the field. Men built that proverbial field, and they own it.

Before women were widely accepted into higher education, the jobs that required degrees were held by men, namely, the people who were encouraged to pursue degrees. (Up through the 1960s, in fact, it was common to see job listings for college science professors that included this caveat: "Women need not apply.")

Working toward gender equality in higher education opened the doors for women to get an education, but not a job. The educational acts of the 1970s were really just the beginning of the bigger push in society to give women equal opportunities in the workforce. Progression in that area would take time.

After the acts were passed, it took time for women to start attending colleges and universities in numbers equal to men. Because of hard-to-break social norms, it was not until we were nearly a decade into the twenty-first century—thirty-five years after the Women's Educational Equity Act was passed—that women surpassed men in terms of college enrollment. And it also took that same amount of time for women to approach men in terms of earning degrees. According to the US Census Bureau, in 2009, among adults twenty-five and older, 29 percent of women had at least a bachelor's degree compared with 30 percent of men (US Census Bureau, 2010a).

In the workforce, women have been closing the gender gap in both *rate of employment* and *income* nearly year after year. During the recession that started in 2008, when job loss was approaching Great Depression numbers, women held onto jobs at much higher rates than did men. Currently, women in full-time jobs make, on average, 20 percent less than do men. However, the number of women in the workforce is on the brink of surpassing the number of men for the first time in American history (Rampell, 2009).

More and more women than ever before have elected to pursue nontraditional roles. Those of us who have chosen to follow careers in math and science know the issues continue well after we complete our schooling. Because of lingering gender stereotypes in the workplace, there still tend to be preconceived notions that a woman's place is not in the STEM disciplines. With time, and possibly as a result of the Baby Boom Generation exiting the workplace, this notion may slowly disappear.

The attrition rate for students enrolled in STEM majors is about the same for women and men. However, since there are dramatically fewer women in STEM majors, our loss is more impactful. Despite the limited number of women who enroll in STEM majors, the overall number of awarded bachelor's degrees has increased significantly in the last four decades. For instance, according to the National Science Foundation (NSF), in 1966 women earned fewer than 5 percent of all bachelor's degrees awarded in physics. In 2006 they earned more than 20 percent. In engineering, women earned .4 percent of bachelor's degrees in 1966. In 2006 they earned more than 19 percent. In chemistry, women went from earning 18 percent of bachelor's degrees in 1966 to earning over half of the degrees awarded in 2006 (National Science Foundation, 2007). These numbers show that we are capable of earning degrees in STEM disciplines. The past forty years also show us that our numbers are slowly improving.

At the college level, many institutions are implementing year-round recruitment programs designed to attract females to STEM programs. While we may have excelled in math and science in high school, we are still less likely than males to choose math and science majors in college. Recruitment programs are aiming to correct this by reaching out to high school females and informing them about the different STEM paths that are available in college and beyond.

Just by recognizing that there is a gender stereotype issue and that it is helping keep female enrollment in STEM majors low, institutions are also raising awareness in their faculties. Instructors at the college level are being asked to self-monitor their behaviors in order to minimize any chance of fostering gender-biased environments. Changes in STEM programs at the college level will hopefully prove to attract and retain more females—both as students and faculty members. Having a male-dominated instructor core does not send the message that the disciplines are equally welcoming to both genders.

Women faculty members in STEM disciplines currently represent the minority, even though their representation has increased slightly with time. The gender gap is even more prevalent among tenured faculty. Despite the gradually rising number of female undergraduate and graduate students, the proportion of women in STEM faculty positions is growing at a much slower pace. There is also a major difference in retention rates among men and women who take on faculty positions in STEM fields. Women faculty members are more likely to leave their positions at higher rates than men (Corbett et al., 2010). This appears to be in part because women, on average, more often report that they are less satisfied with their faculty jobs than men. Of course, job satisfaction is a major influencer for staying in a position. According to the NSF, some of the main reasons women cite as leading to their job dissatisfaction include unclear institutional policies and practices, isolation, and lack of mentoring. The only long-term solution for fixing the problem of women faculty members leaving their careers is to address and correct the problems cited by women faculty members themselves.

In an attempt to correct these problems, the NSF has implemented the ADVANCE Program, which aims to increase the advancement of women in science and engineering careers within academia. ADVANCE "focuses on ensuring that women faculty with earned STEM degrees consider academia as a viable and attractive career option" (National Science Foundation, 2010).

In disciplines such as computer science, mathematics, physics, and engineering, female faculty members are in short supply. So, attracting and retaining female faculty is important to help with efforts in recruiting and retaining female students. One possible reason that women avoid faculty positions is that the women who choose to explore STEM disciplines are less likely to be interested in a traditionally female career such as teaching. However, teaching higher education and becoming tenured have not been common paths for women in the past.

For progress to occur in STEM programs on campuses, institution administrators must understand the reasons that the programs are not attracting and retaining female faculty members. Remember, it was not even forty years ago that Congress passed the Women's Educational Equity Act that provided federal protection against gender discrimination in educational settings. In such a short amount of time, we cannot expect our fellow women to earn graduate degrees, pursue STEM faculty positions, *and* fill as many academic positions as men do. The Women's Educational Equity Act forced the educational floodgates open for women. However, not all of us who were interested in higher education rushed into the STEM fields, which were, and still are, viewed as masculine fields. But the culture of STEM field programs is changing. As more and more of us pursue and acquire faculty positions at various universities, the culture of the STEM fields will become more and more inviting to all women.

The fact still remains that women in STEM careers have higher attrition rates than do their male coworkers *and* women in careers outside of the STEM disciplines. Addressing the reasons why the attrition rates are drastically higher is important for starting the discussion and correcting the problem. Researchers are exploring other factors that possibly overwhelm women in STEM fields, including extreme work schedules, more frequent disciplinary actions, or unclear rules about advancement.

Women are gaining numbers in traditionally male-dominated fields, but they are still significantly outnumbered in STEM occupations. Men drastically outnumber women in terms of bachelor's degrees awarded in STEM fields, which is a direct result of more men enrolling in STEM majors overall. Addressing these problems has been the first step in finding solutions. Getting talented women into male-dominated careers is one struggle, while keeping them there is another. This issue is especially apparent in STEM careers, which are extremely important to the global economy.

The NSF estimates that between 4 and 5 percent of the global workforce works directly in science, engineering, and technology. This relatively small group of workers, about five million people, is critical to improving the global economy. Attracting and retaining more women in STEM careers will help tremendously to improve diversity, maximize creativity, and boost competitiveness.

Likewise, attracting and retaining women in the fields that today remain dominated by males is important for the advancement of those fields. Women bring a different perspective to the workplace and can help breed creativity in scientific fields that can only expand as broadly as the minds that work within them. The number of women employed in STEM fields has increased over the last few decades, but not at rates that will soon eliminate the domination in those fields by males. Gender bias on the job is still prevalent in the workforce, although not in the same overt ways it was in the past. In order to limit gender biases, employers need to monitor their hiring practices, their work environments, and the ways in which they might be hindering gender diversity.

As our society as a whole improves at treating careers as gender neutral, boys and girls alike will be able to see all careers as possible opportunities. By no means will all women suddenly rush into STEM fields, which is not the point at all. Young boys and girls should be allowed to follow their interests without lingering social stigmas. Possibly more than any other area, the STEM fields will greatly benefit from a more balanced male-to-female ratio. Many jobs within the STEM fields focus on designing products and materials that aim to advance our experiences and allow us to live safer lives. Therefore, it is critical to have a strong female presence to ensure that products and materials are developed to benefit both genders. Without the involvement of women in these fields, product designers may easily overlook needs that are specific to women. Examples of this are evident in the design of past products. For instance, when voice-recognition was first becoming popular, the systems were calibrated to recognize male voices because only males were designing the products. Because of this, women's voices were unrecognized when they tried to use the various systems.

A similar, albeit potentially more dangerous, case happened within the automobile industry. When engineers designed the first automotive air bags, they fit the body dimensions of the team, which was composed primarily of adult males. Therefore, when the air bags deployed in an accident, those with smaller body sizes, such as children and the majority of women, were at risk. Including capable female engineers on the design team could have helped avoid this mistake.

Having people with different mind-sets, capabilities, and imaginations on production teams improves the creative process and helps minimize avoidable mistakes. Products rooted in science and technology are likely to better meet the needs of both men and women if the products are designed by teams composed of both genders. It is a matter of designing products that are compatible with a broad audience; it is a matter of safety; and it starts with attracting more women into STEM careers.

As women become more prevalent in STEM careers, more and more young girls will begin to recognize the additional career opportunities open to them. With more women in the field, it will become more evident to young girls what they, as engineers, can offer the world. Without being able to see this link, they will continue to have problems seeing certain positions as viable possibilities, even if they have some intrinsic interest in the subject matter. If girls cannot visualize themselves in STEM careers because they have never seen women in those positions, they will be much less likely to ever use their innate aptitudes and abilities in a math- or science-oriented specialty. That will truly be a loss of gigantic proportion.

For inspiration, tools, and resources, visit www.UnlockingYourBrilliance.com and www.STEMspire.org.

CONCLUSION

I could have called this chapter "Follow Your Path, Regardless of How Many Men Are in the Room." And in so doing, it would have brought me back to the memorable trip I made in 2010 to Seattle and Vancouver, which you'll recall that I mentioned in the preface of this book. That experience gave me an opportunity to reflect on my professional life in a way I hadn't done before. In telling my trusted friends my story, I realized that I had followed my path regardless of, and in part because of, how many men had joined me in classrooms, meeting rooms, boardrooms, and conference rooms.

By the time of the EO forum's retreat, being surrounded by men had become common practice, so I was not uneasy or completely naïve. I learned about the members individually and also a lot about men collectively. I had never had the chance to share my story with a group of men, and I was flattered that they found my professional past impressive.

For the remainder of the trip, whenever one of the men would do something typically "man-like," he almost always instinctively followed it by saying, "Don't put that in your book."

That memorable 2010 retreat turned out to be a once-in-a-life-time experience. I will never forget the conversation I had during the limo ride back to the United States from the Olympics. It, as well as the remainder of the trip, strengthened the relationship we EO members had as a forum and the friendships between individuals. These men have continued to provide unconditional support for my company, my nonprofit, and me. I recently learned that I won the 2012 *Reno Gazette-Journal* Entrepreneur of the Year award for a medium-size company. My forum members were the first ones to congratulate me and to say they would be at the awards dinner to support me. I have found the confidence, respect, and support needed to thrive in a STEM field. I hope that you will too!

BIBLIOGRAPHY

Baumgartner-Papageorgiou, Alice. "'My Daddy Might Have Loved Me': Student Perceptions of Differences Between Being Male and Being Female." Institute for Equality in Education, University of Colorado at Denver (1982, 1992). Retrieved from www.eric.ed.gov/PDFS/ED221436.pdf.

Corbett, C., C. Hill, and A. St. Rose. "Why So Few?: Women in Science, Technology, Engineering and Mathematics." Washington, DC: American Association of University Women (2010). Retrieved from www.aauw.org/learn/research/upload/whysofew.pdf.

Dyer, Susan K., ed. "Under the Microscope: A Decade of Gender Equity Projects in the Sciences." American Association of University Women Educational Foundation, Washington, DC (2004).

Farmer, Lesley S.J. "Technology + Girls = An Equal Chance for Success" (2009). Retrieved from www.pta.org/3737.htm.

Georgetown University Center on Education and the Workforce. "Highest Proportion of Science, Engineering, Tech, and Math Jobs in DC." Georgetown University website (October 20, 2011). Retrieved from www.georgetown.edu/story/cew-report-science -technology-math-jobs.html.

Girl Scouts of the USA (2012). Retrieved from www.girlscouts. org.

Hewlett, Sylvia Ann. *The Athena Factor: Reversing the Brain Drain in Science, Engineering, and Technology.* Boston: Harvard Business School (2008).

Hunt, J. "Why Do Women Leave Science and Engineering?" *Forbes* (2010). Retrieved from www.forbes.com/2010/06/08/science-engineering-gender-gap-forbes-woman-leadership-pay-promotion.html.

Institute for Mathematics and Computer Science (IMACS). "Keeping Talented Girls on the STEM Track" (September 8, 2011). Retrieved from www.eimacs.com/blog/?p=448.

Lade, Jennifer. "Local Programs Steer Girls Toward Science." *The New England Business Bulletin* (July 2011). Retrieved from www.southcoasttoday.com/apps/pbcs.dll/article?AID=/20110722/NEBULLETIN/108010307/1036.

Lewin, Tamar. "Bias Called Persistent Hurdle for Women in Sciences." *New York Times* (March 22, 2010). Retrieved from www.nytimes.com/2010/03/22/science/22women.html.

"Lisa P. Jackson." Wikipedia, the Free Encyclopedia (2012). Retrieved from en.wikipedia.org/wiki/Lisa_P._Jackson.

National Science Foundation. "Women, Minorities, and Persons with Disabilities in Science and Engineering." NSF 07-315 (Arlington, VA, February 2007).

National Science Foundation (2010). Retrieved from www.nsf.gov.

Rampell, C. "As Layoffs Surge, Women May Pass Men in Job Force." *The New York Times* (February 2009). Retrieved from www.nytimes.com/2009/02/06/business/06women.html.

Society of Women Engineers. "Attitudes and Experiences of Engineering Alumni." Harris Interactive Market Research (2006).

US Census Bureau, Current Population Survey 2009. (2010a). "Census Bureau Reports Nearly 6 in 10 Advanced Degree Holders Age 25-29 Are Women." Retrieved from www.census.gov /newsroom/releases/archives/education/cb10-55.html.

US Census Bureau, Current Population Survey 2009. (2010b). "Census Bureau Reports Families with Children Increasingly Face Unemployment." Retrieved from www.census.gov/news room/releases/archives/families_households/cb10-08.html.

US Department of Labor, Office of the Assistant Secretary for Administration and Management (2010). Title IX of the Education Amendments of 1972, 20 U.S.C, 1681-1688 (2010). Retrieved from www.dol.gov/oasam/regs/statutes/titleix.htm.

US Economics and Statistics Administration. "Women in STEM: A Gender Gap to Innovation" (2011). Calculations from American Community Survey public-use microdata.

Wiest, L. R. "Out-of-School-Time (OST) Programs as Mathematics Support for Females." *International Perspectives on Gender and Mathematics Education* (2011), 55-86.

ABOUT THE AUTHOR

Karen Purcell, PE, is a dynamic engineer, entrepreneur, and author focused on helping young women connect the dots to a meaningful future in the STEM fields. She draws on her successful engineering experience to inspire young women to enter into math-, technology-, and science-related careers with full confidence, knowing that she did it, other women have done it, and they—today's gifted STEM majors—are unquestionably our leaders of tomorrow. They can succeed, take advantage of tremendous growth opportunities, and lead the way in STEM while helping our country thrive in the twenty-first century.

Karen is the founder, owner, and president of PK Electrical, an eighteen-person electrical engineering firm. She is actively involved in the Reno/Tahoe chapter of the Entrepreneurs' Organization and has held numerous officer positions for the last six years. Most recently, she was the chapter's president.

Karen holds a bachelor of science degree in electrical engineering from Widener University in Pennsylvania. She is an avid runner of half marathons, a Girl Scout troop leader, and a volunteer with Big Brothers, Big Sisters. She and her husband have two daughters.

Karen received the 2012 *Reno Gazette-Journal*'s Entrepreneur of the Year award for a medium-size company. The annual award celebrates individuals and companies that have significantly enhanced the growth and prestige of the technology community in northern Nevada and recognizes outstanding leaders at all levels of business.

CONNECT, JOIN, AND LEAD

Take a moment to connect with Karen Purcell and join the conversation to help lead the movement of women into the science, technology, engineering and math (STEM) fields. We would love your support and welcome your participation!

- Follow Karen on Twitter @STEMspire and become her fan on Facebook.com.
- For more free downloads, tools, and resources and to sign up for her newsletter, visit www.UnlockingYourBrilliance.com.
- To Book Karen for a speaking engagement, please contact her team at info@unlockingyourbrilliance.com.

A portion of the proceeds of this book will go toward nonprofit organizations dedicated to helping women advance in the STEM fields.

ABOUT STEM

Karen Purcell founded the nonprofit organization STEMspire to provide education, encouragement, inspiration, and financial resources to help more young women pursue careers in the STEM fields. Visit STEMspire.org for more information or to make a donation.